The Big6™ Curriculum

The Big6™ Curriculum:
Comprehensive Information and Communication Technology (ICT) Literacy for All Students

Michael B. Eisenberg, Janet Murray, and Colet Bartow

LIBRARIES
UNLIMITED™
An Imprint of ABC-CLIO, LLC
Santa Barbara, California • Denver, Colorado

Copyright © 2016 by ABC-CLIO, LLC

Library of Congress Cataloging-in-Publication Data

Names: Eisenberg, Michael B., 1949– | Murray, Janet R., 1946– author. | Bartow, Colet, author.

Title: The Big6 curriculum : comprehensive information and communication technology (ICT) literacy for all students / Michael B. Eisenberg, Janet Murray, and Colet Bartow.

Description: Santa Barbara, CA : Libraries Unlimited, [2016] | Includes bibliographical references.

Identifiers: LCCN 2015049680 (print) | LCCN 2016015974 (ebook) | ISBN 9781440844799 (pbk : acid-free paper) | ISBN 9781440844805 (eBook)

Subjects: LCSH: Information literacy—Study and teaching. | Electronic information resource literacy—Study and teaching. | Information technology—Study and teaching.

Classification: LCC ZA3075 .E383 2016 (print) | LCC ZA3075 (ebook) | DDC 028.7071—dc23

LC record available at https://lccn.loc.gov/2015049680

ISBN: 978-1-4408-4479-9
EISBN: 978-1-4408-4480-5

20 19 18 17 16   1 2 3 4 5

This book is also available as an eBook.

Libraries Unlimited
An Imprint of ABC-CLIO, LLC

ABC-CLIO, LLC
130 Cremona Drive, P.O. Box 1911
Santa Barbara, California 93116-1911
www.abc-clio.com

This book is printed on acid-free paper ∞
Manufactured in the United States of America

To Sue Wurster,
in appreciation for all your contributions;
this one's for you!

CONTENTS

LIST OF FIGURES

Chapter 1

BIG6™ BY THE MONTH:
A SWEEPING NEW APPROACH
TO ICT LITERACY LEARNING!

In This Chapter

❏ Rationale for a Comprehensive Program

❏ The Big6™ and Super3™

❏ Defined

❏ Predictable

❏ Measured

❏ Reported

❏ Summary

Rationale for a Comprehensive Program: Achieving Comprehensive Information and Communication Technology (ICT) Literacy

This is a practical, hands-on book about how to create an instructional program in your school that ensures every student is information and communication technology (ICT) literate—able to define information needs and use a range of tools, technologies, and techniques to search, locate, use, and apply information to meet those needs.

There is little argument about the value and importance of ICT literacy, with references, articles, and discussions in the media and on the web related to some form of information and technology almost every day. There's also general agreement about the information and communication technology skills, abilities, and understandings that comprise ICT literacy. We see this agreement in the form of white papers and policy documents by various organizations and government agencies, as well as in the curriculum and standards developed at the national, state, and local levels.

So, what's the problem? Why do we need a "sweeping new approach" to ICT literacy educational programs?

The sad truth is that few, if any, ICT literacy efforts in schools have fulfilled the promise of a *comprehensive* program—one that reaches all students.

The problem is that while many praise ICT literacy, almost all ICT literacy educational programs can be characterized as irregular, partial, incomplete, or arbitrary. Certainly some students receive excellent information literacy instruction, but others receive little or none. Many classroom teachers, teacher-librarians, and technology teachers offer excellent lessons on specific skills, tools, or techniques, but very few schools or districts offer a complete program, with clearly defined goals and objectives, planned and coordinated instruction, regular and objective assessment of learning, and formal reporting of results.

The reasons for this situation are varied and understandable. In some cases there are insufficient staff or limited resources. Lack of space or routine access to technology may be problems. And ICT literacy doesn't fit nicely into the current curricular structure of most schools. Information and communication technology literacy crosses the boundaries of various subjects and disciplines; it's not fully subsumed under one of the traditional, established curriculum areas.

Most telling, the main reason for irregular or incomplete programs is that the ICT literacy program is not viewed in most schools as a vital part of the school's curriculum program; information literacy is not treated as essential for every student in the same way as reading, writing, science, math, or social studies.

This nonessential status must end! In the 21st century, reading and writing are no longer sufficient for success in school and work. To succeed in our global, information society, students must be able to find and use information in all its forms as well as produce and present it in all forms. That's ICT literacy, and any student who graduates without these skills is at a serious disadvantage.

It's time to turn this around—and that's the purpose of this book: to accept the challenge of ensuring that every student is ICT literate:

To fulfill the promise of providing *comprehensive* information and communication technology literacy programs for every student in every school.

A comprehensive ICT literacy program should reach all students in the school:

- A comprehensive program must be clearly *defined* in terms of the goals and specific skills and knowledge that students are expected to learn.
- A comprehensive program must be *predictable* in terms of how and when students are to learn the defined, essential information and technology skills and knowledge.
- A comprehensive program must be *measurable* in terms of setting accountable goals for the program and assessing performance by the students.
- A comprehensive program must *report* the results—to students and parents, and to other teachers, administrators, and decision makers.

A major emphasis of the Big6 by the Month approach is practical, planned, and accountable instruction. Every information literacy lesson and learning activity—whether based in the classroom, library, or technology lab—must be linked to the goals, objectives, and standards defined in the school-wide plan as well as tied to classroom assignments and curriculum.

The actual instructional Big6 by the Month program must be realistic, with goals, objectives, and standards that are attainable because they match the time and effort that can be allocated by teacher-librarians, classroom teachers, technology teachers, and others to the program. The scope and depth of the program is directly related to instructional time and effort available.

Big6 by the Month ICT Literacy Program	=	Time and effort of teacher-librarians, classroom teachers, tech support, others

As stated, ICT literacy is too important to be arbitrary or irregular. However, the scope and depth of the program in individual schools or districts will vary—particularly in the beginning—because each has unique requirements, resources, and infrastructure to assign to that program. The ultimate goal is for every student to attain the full set of information and communication technology skills and understandings. The practicality and flexibility of the Big6 by the Month approach will allow schools and districts to start immediately and then adjust and expand as the value is recognized and more assets are allocated.

The Big6™ and Super3™

In order to develop and deliver ICT literacy programs that are comprehensive (will reach all users), predictable (are consistent over time), and accountable (can be measured and reported), we developed Big6 by the Month. The program is based on the Big6 approach to information problem-solving, the most widely used model and approach to ICT literacy in the world.

Developed by information literacy educators Mike Eisenberg and Bob Berkowitz, the Big6 is the most widely known and widely used information literacy approach to teaching information and technology skills in the world. The Big6 is an information and technology literacy model and curriculum, implemented in thousands of schools, K through higher education. Some people call the Big6 an information problem-solving strategy, because with the Big6 students are able to handle any problem, assignment, decision, or task. Figure 1.1 shows the six stages we call the Big6. Two substages are part of each main category in the Big6 model.

Students go through these Big6 stages—consciously or not—when they seek or apply information to solve a problem or make a decision. It's not necessary to complete these stages in a linear order, and a given stage doesn't have to take a lot of time. We have found that almost all successful problem-solving situations address all stages.

Thousands of students around the world have learned and used the Big6 and the specific skills and knowledge within the Big6 process. The Big6 is applicable in any information problem-solving situation: school, play, and work. The Big6 is flexible and easily integrated with classroom activities and assignments.

However, not every student has the opportunity to learn and use the Big6—or any other information problem-solving process. As emphasized above, even though there is widespread recognition of the importance of information and technology literacy, few schools or districts have "comprehensive" programs that reach every student. That's why we need a Big6 by the Month program.

The Big6™

1. Task Definition
    1.1 Define the information problem
    1.2 Identify information needed

2. Information Seeking Strategies
    2.1 Determine all possible sources
    2.2 Select the best sources

3. Location & Access
    3.1 Locate sources (intellectually and physically)
    3.2 Find information within sources

4. Use of Information
    4.1 Engage (e.g., read, hear, view, touch)
    4.2 Extract relevant information

5. Synthesis
    5.1 Organize from multiple sources
    5.2 Present the information

6. Evaluation
    6.1 Judge the product (effectiveness)
    6.2 Judge the process (efficiency)

Figure 1.1 The Big6™ Model of Information Problem Solving

Educators working with young students (pre-K to grade 2) may prefer to base their ICT literacy programs on the Super3 (Plan—Do—Review) rather than the Big6.

The Super3 (see Figure 1.2) is the "pre-Big6" model of information problem-solving for very young children. The Super3 is a familiar, easy-to-remember, three-stage process for doing anything: a classroom task, an assignment, homework, a project, or even a fun activity. Like the Big6, the Super3 is widely applicable—to schoolwork, recreation, or decision making in kids' personal lives (e.g., what birthday present to get mom, what game to play with a friend).

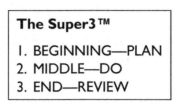

The Super3™

1. BEGINNING—PLAN
2. MIDDLE—DO
3. END—REVIEW

Figure 1.2 The Super3™

Students are able to easily transition from the Super3 to the Big6, as they are both representations of the same information problem-solving process (see Figure 1.3). Students engaging in PLAN are accomplishing Big6 stages 1 and 2, Task Definition and Information Seeking Strategies. Super3 stage DO encompasses the three middle stages of the Big6, the stages in which students actively engage in the work of solving the task: 3, Location & Access; 4, Use of Information; and 5, Synthesis. The last Super3 stage, REVIEW, aligns directly with Big6 stage 6, Evaluation.

Super3™	Big6™
PLAN	Task Definition
	Information Seeking Strategies
DO	Location & Access
	Use of Information
	Synthesis
REVIEW	Evaluation

Figure 1.3 Super3™–Big6™ Alignment

In our Big6 work, we've always emphasized being systematic and flexible—being organized, practical, and integrating with other instructional priorities and plans. But now, due to the demands placed on students by our information- and technology-intensive world, it's time to be even more ambitious: to strive for comprehensive ICT literacy that helps every student attain the skills and knowledge to thrive in school and society.

That's the purpose of the Big6 by the Month program. It is a four-element strategy that, if followed, all but guarantees a successful information and technology literacy program. Here are the four elements:

- **Defined**: Identify essential, "power" learning objectives/grade level expectations for each Big6/Super3 skill at each grade level. Link to standards (subject area, Common Core, information literacy, ICT).

- **Predictable**: Implement a consistent, intentional, monthly program coordinated and integrated with classroom curriculum.

- **Measured**: Identify assessment criteria, strategies, and evidence for each Big6 grade level expectation.

- **Reported**: Identify formal reporting mechanisms (to students, other teachers, administrators, parents).

Each of these four elements is explained in more detail below.

Defined

Comprehensive ICT literacy requires a clear understanding of goals. This means that the first requirements of the program are to

- identify essential, "power" ICT literacy goals and learning objectives for all students in your school; and
- develop grade-level objectives for each Big6 skill at each grade level. Link these goals and objectives to relevant national or local learning standards.

However, **do not overreach**!!

Define goals and objectives that are **ambitious but attainable**. Remember, these goals and objectives need to be comprehensive—intended for every student. We recommend starting with two to four "power learning objectives" for each Big6 stage for each grade level for each month, as our challenge is to reach all students rather than providing in-depth learning for just one or a few classes.

In later chapters, we share many resources for identifying possible "power" learning objectives. Information literacy was formally defined and recognized as a priority by the American Library Association in 1989, and there are many well-developed conceptualizations of the nature and scope of ICT literacy, including the following:

American Association of School Librarians, AASL. (2007). *AASL Standards for the 21st-Century Learner*. http://www.ala.org/aasl/standards

Association of College and Research Libraries, ACRL. (2008). "Information Literacy Competency Standards for Higher Education." http://www.ala.org/ala/mgrps/divs/acrl/standards/informationliteracycompetency.cfm

International Society for Technology in Education, ISTE. (2007). National Educational Technology Standards for Students (2nd ed.). http://www.iste.org/standards

Kent State University Libraries. (2010). TRAILS: Tools for Real-Time Assessment of Information Literacy Skills. http://www.trails-9.org/

Partnership for 21st Century Skills, P21. (2003). *Learning for the 21st Century*. http://www.p21.org/index.php

The AASL and ACRL standards are based on conceptualizations and experiences of librarians over many years. Together, they cover pre-K through higher education and are very useful for identifying specific subskills under each of the Big6 stages. The ISTE NETS-S standards represent the best thinking of educators engaged with using technology for learning and teaching. TRAILS is an online information literacy assessment program that seeks to measure performance on information literacy items based on AASL and the Common Core. P21 is a broad-based, national effort including educational organizations and businesses dedicated to providing guidance and support so that all students gain essential 21st-century skills. These resources provide a rich base of ideas for identifying and defining the key power standards and learning objectives for each Big6 stage.

Of course, the most recent identification and highlighting of key information literacy skills is found in the Common Core State Standards Initiative (http://www.corestandards.org/about-the-standards) in writing, reading, and mathematics, and applied to history/social studies, science, and technical subjects, adopted by most states. The Common Core State Standards seek to define the knowledge and skills students should gain, K–12, to succeed after high school in the workplace, higher education, or workforce training programs. The Common Core is a set of goals, objectives, and standards, not a fully developed curriculum. The Big6 by the Month program is able to use the Common Core standards and put them into practice.

Predictable

The main purpose of focusing on one Big6 (or Super3) stage each month is to be able to more easily plan and implement a consistent, intentional program that reaches every student. Here, too, the program should be ambitious but also practical. Certain overarching logistical questions guide the predictable part of the program:

How can we reach all students?

How much time and effort can classroom teachers, teacher-librarians, technology teachers, and others devote to the program?

What are the key assignments and curriculum units to link to?

The Big6 by the Month Literacy Program is *predictable* in that there is a specific Big6 or Super3 stage taught and learned each month, and the skills and knowledge learned build from month to month and grade to grade. The monthly Big6 plan should work smoothly with the calendar, organization, and schedule of the school and district. Context is essential—highlighting the connections to the overall Big6 or Super3 process and to subject area curriculum. Big6 and Super3 lessons and activities fully integrate with classroom curriculum and assignments. Each month, our approach is to identify one or two assignments for each teacher in each grade level, then develop lessons targeted to those assignments.

This approach is not meant to constrict or constrain. You can still offer a lesson or activity on a different Big6 skill in any given month. But it does mean that the monthly emphasis is on the main skill designated for that month (within the context of an assignment or curriculum topic).

The recommended Big6 by the Month calendar appears in Figure 1.4. This calendar can be adjusted for individual schools or districts, but we encourage schools and educators to try to follow a consistent schedule. In this way, the program is predictable. And if we all do this—across the globe—we can share ideas, objectives, lessons, activities, and assessments. It also means that we can work together to publicize and promote the ICT literacy program.

This Big6 by the Month schedule should work for most schools and districts because it is built around grade level and month and not individual classes or teachers. There are clearly defined learning objectives and assessments for students in each grade level, while specific lessons and learning activities are customized for each setting. The monthly focus remains consistent: having every student in a particular grade attain clearly defined skills and knowledge for a specific Big6 stage.

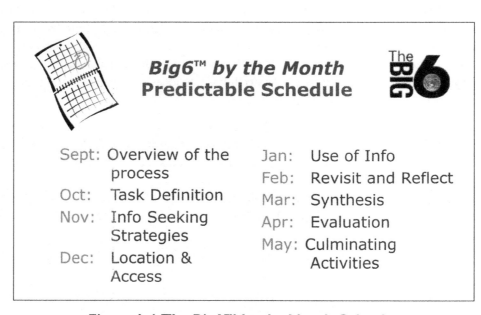

Big6™ by the Month Predictable Schedule The BIG 6

Sept: Overview of the process

Oct: Task Definition

Nov: Info Seeking Strategies

Dec: Location & Access

Jan: Use of Info

Feb: Revisit and Reflect

Mar: Synthesis

Apr: Evaluation

May: Culminating Activities

Figure 1.4 The Big6™ by the Month Calendar

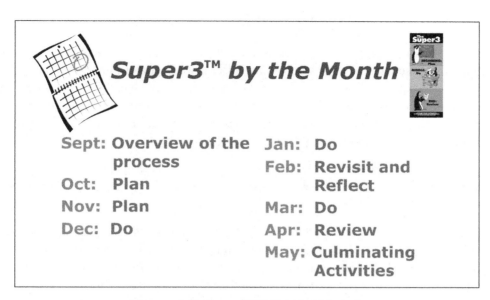

Figure 1.5 Super3™ by the Month

However, the schedule can be adjusted by a school or district depending on the organizational calendar of instruction. For example, schools on a year-round model may want to spread out the program over 12 months, or a school with a strong semester structure may choose to plan to cover all six Big6 stages within a semester, repeating them twice during the school year.

Figure 1.5 shows a Super3 by the Month schedule, consistent with the Big6 by the Month schedule described above, spending two months on each of the Super3 stages. That will allow students to become very comfortable with the terminology and the actions to take for each.

Alternatively, considering the attention span and needs of young children, teachers may prefer shorter segments, cycling through the Super3 process twice during the school year. Figure 1.6 shows how that calendar might work.

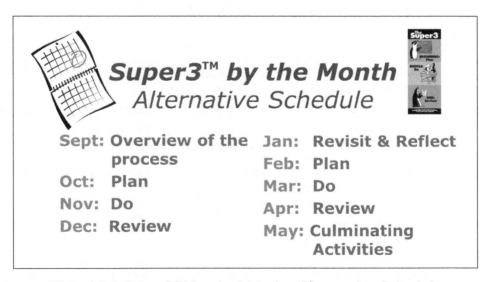

Figure 1.6 Super3™ by the Month—Alternative Schedule

Measured

The Big6 by the Month program calls for measurement on two levels: student performance and program effectiveness and efficiency. Students and their teachers need to be able to determine if they have achieved the desired goals and objectives. Parents and administrators also need to be kept abreast of progress. On a program level, educators want to know whether the program is successful in meeting the goals and objectives of a comprehensive ICT literacy program as well as how well the structure, organization, and time and effort of the program are working. Both levels of assessment will inform adjustments and future planning.

Details of specific student assessments targeted to specific Big6 and Super3 skills are presented in subsequent chapters. Assessment should not be onerous for students or burdensome for teachers. We streamline measurement by focusing on two aspects: evidence and criteria.

Evidence of student learning includes observation, student-teacher interactions, student assignments, projects, and formal testing. Evidence can be collected from actions and products that students are already engaged in for other curricular work (including school, district, or statewide exams) or from specifically designed ICT literacy assessments, including projects, reports, and formal assessments such as TRAILS (Kent State University Libraries 2010; see above).

Evidence is analyzed in terms of *criteria*: benchmarks that reflect achievement in relation to stated learning objectives. Common ICT criteria include quality, accuracy, completeness, logical reasoning, writing (or presentation), insightfulness, and creativity.

Reported

The final piece of the comprehensive ICT literacy program is reporting: communicating about the program and student performance. Student performance information should be shared with the students themselves as well as parents, teachers, and appropriate others. Descriptions and insights about the nature, scope, and effectiveness of the information literacy program are provided for the faculty, building or district leadership groups, administration, school board, and community.

We believe it's particularly important to provide information about the value and importance of ICT literacy as well as the specifics of student learning within the Big6 by the Month program to parents via a monthly report or newsletter. This can be delivered in print, via e-mail, or online. In later chapters, we provide specific guidelines and examples of how to create meaningful reports for parents that don't require extensive time commitments.

Summary

The overarching purpose of the Big6 by the Month program is to deliver on the promise and importance of ICT literacy for all students. Big6 by the Month allows educators to take a fully comprehensive view of problems, lessons, learning, thinking skills, planning, standards, and assessment. To our knowledge, no other program offers such an organized and far-reaching perspective to scaffold problem-solving skill expertise among the student population. No other program aims to reach every student with a systematic and unified approach.

In past generations, a student could memorize and repeat facts to be successful in school, life, and work. This is no longer the case. Students today and in the future will need to solve many and varied problems by sizing up a situation, identifying and gathering relevant and credible information, applying and presenting information and knowledge to others in understandable ways, and assessing their own products and competencies. They will need to think creatively and flexibly to adjust to a swiftly changing environment and social conditions.

The Big6 by the Month plan equips schools and districts to enable students to learn and use information problem-solving skills to thrive in school, personal life, and eventually the workforce in a rapidly changing world.

Chapter 2

BIG6™ BY THE MONTH

September:
Program Overview

In This Chapter

- ❑ Developing a Big6™ by the Month Program
- ❑ Defined: Standards and Grade Level Objectives
- ❑ Predictable: Schedule and Instruction
- ❑ Measured: Types of Assessment; Samples of Evidence and Criteria
- ❑ Reported: Audience and Format
- ❑ Summary
- ❑ Online Resources

Developing a Big6™ by the Month Program

After Mike Eisenberg published a "white paper" on the Big6 by the Month idea (see Chapter 1) in August 2010, he assembled a professional Big6 team to plan, expand, and present the Big6 by the Month monthly webinar program:

- **Janet Murray** is a retired teacher-librarian and the author of *Achieving Educational Standards Using the Big6™*.
- **Colet Bartow** is the Content Standards Coordinator for the Montana Office of Public Instruction.
- **Sue Wurster** is the Project Manager and Executive Director of Big6 Associates, LLC.
- **Mike Eisenberg** is Dean Emeritus of the iSchool at the University of Washington and cofounder of the Big6 Skills.

See "About the Authors" in the back of the book for more detail.

This book collects and presents the monthly webinar content following three years of live webinar presentations and revisions. Big6 by the Month is designed to be useful to all educators: classroom teachers, teacher-librarians, technology teachers, and administrators. The word "you" refers to you, the reader, as you explore and adapt the strategies we have developed. The glossary in the back of the book defines the educational terms we have used; those terms are italicized when first used in the text.

Big6 by the Month offers the conceptual and practical foundation to help you plan and deliver an *information and communication technology (ICT) literacy* (see glossary) instructional program that is comprehensive (will reach all users), predictable (is consistent over time), and accountable (can be measured and reported). There are four essential elements:

- **Defined**: Identify essential, *"power"* grade level objectives/learning expectations for each Big6/Super3™ skill at each grade level. Link objectives or learning expectations to standards (subject area, information literacy, ICT).

- **Predictable**: Implement a consistent, intentional, monthly program coordinated and integrated with classroom curriculum.

- **Measured**: Identify assessment criteria, strategies, and evidence for each Big6 grade level expectation.

- **Reported**: Identify formal reporting mechanisms (to students, other teachers, administrators, parents).

Each individual school or district should develop a customized Big6 by the Month (B6xM) program based on all four elements—defined, predictable, measured, and reported. The overall program uses these four elements to set the annual scope and structure of the program. Then, we again use the four elements to plan, develop, and implement instruction pertaining to the Big6 focus for that month (e.g., Task Definition in October, Information Seeking Strategies in November).

We recommend that you plan and prepare all four elements at least a month ahead in order to connect ideas to the school's calendar and anticipated classroom curriculum.

For each month's Big6 topic, identify specific, attainable *grade level objectives* and make the connection to related *content standards*, *information literacy* standards, and technology standards. Then sketch out instructional lessons for each grade level along with appropriate assessment techniques and strategies. Finally, report monthly results to the students, other teachers, administrators, and parents.

For more web links to relevant resources for each Big6 stage and a discussion group (http://groups.google.com /group/b6month?hl=en) at which you can ask questions and share your instructional strategies, check out the Big6 by the Month Google site: http://sites.google.com/site/big6xthemonth/home.

Defined

Standards

Standards describe what students need to *know* and be able to *do*. Colet Bartow created the chart shown in Figure 2.1 to clearly differentiate between those two parts of the definition of standards.

The Big6 Skills is an information problem-solving *process* that focuses instruction on the skills students need to be *able to do* (see the *"Able to Do"* column in the figure).

Know = Content Specific	*Able to Do =* Process and Performance
Mathematics (facts and formulas)	Problem Solving
Social Studies (names, dates, places)	Problem Solving and Research
Science (facts and formulas)	Inquiry, Process, Practices
Literature	Reading, Writing, Listening, Speaking

Colet Bartow, Big6 by the Month (2012).

Figure 2.1 Standards—Knowledge and Process

A variety of organizations have developed ICT literacy standards. The American Association of School Librarians articulated *Standards for the 21st-Century Learner* (http://www.ala.org/aasl/standards/learning). The Association for College and Research Libraries has also published "Information Literacy Competency Standards for Higher

Education" (http://www.ala.org/ala/mgrps/divs/acrl/standards/informationliteracycompetency.cfm), which may be a useful reference with secondary students. The TRAILS site (http://www.trails-9.org/) gives us an independent tool to help students evaluate their information literacy skills in five categories. ISTE's National Educational Technology Standards (NETS) for Students (http://www.iste.org/standards) delineates six categories of standards, one of which is "Research and Information Fluency," described as follows:

Students apply digital tools to gather, evaluate, and use information. Students:

- plan strategies to guide inquiry.
- locate, organize, analyze, evaluate, synthesize, and ethically use information from a variety of sources and media.
- evaluate and select information sources and digital tools based on the appropriateness to specific tasks.
- process data and report results.

Other standards in the categories "Critical Thinking, Problem Solving and Decision Making" and "Communication and Collaboration" are also relevant to the standards presented in Big6 by the Month webinars.

Teachers and students need to know that information literacy and technology skills are important in all areas of the curriculum, not just as part of research or "library skills" or "computer skills."

The Common Core State Standards Initiative (http://corestandards.org/) provides a national set of guidelines to describe what high school graduates must know and be able to do in order to succeed in entry-level college courses or the workplace. Examine your state's *content standards* to find standards that relate to ICT literacy. (Use the *Standards Template*. See the "Templates" section in the appendices at the end of this book or online in the Files at the Big6 by the Month Google site, https://sites.google.com/site/big6xthemonth/file-cabinet.)

Grade Level Objectives

The Big6 by the Month program is organized to offer in-depth instruction on one major Big6 stage each month. We recommend analyzing national, state, and local standards and curriculum to identify the ones that are most important (in your situation) for each Big6 stage, then selecting the essential, "power" information literacy goals and learning objectives for students in each grade level in your school. See Figure 2.2.

Use the *Grade Level Objectives Template* to identify learning expectations for each grade level.

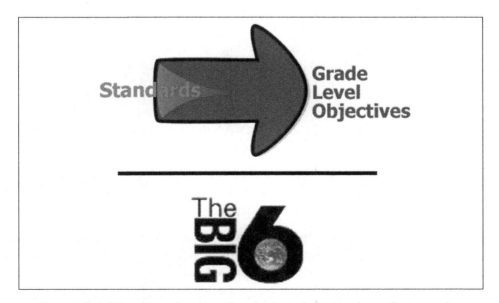

Figure 2.2 The Standards—Grade Level Objectives Connection

Predictable

For each month of the academic year, there is an instructional Big6 by the Month focus for school-wide information literacy learning. The proposed school year schedule—September through May—is outlined in Figure 2.3.

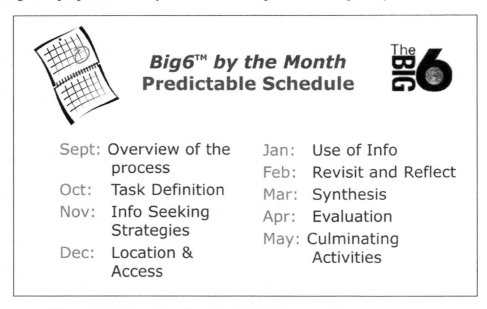

Figure 2.3 The Predictable Big6™ by the Month Schedule

The Schedule

This nine-month plan may not work for every school or district depending on the organizational calendar of instruction. For example, schools on a year-round model may want to spread out the program over 12 months, or a school with a strong semester structure may choose to plan to cover all six Big6 stages within a semester.

A nine-month Big6 by the Month approach should work for most schools and districts because it is built around grade level and month and not individual classes or teachers. There are clearly defined learning objectives and assessments for students in each grade level, while specific lessons and learning activities are customized for each setting. The monthly focus remains consistent: having every student in a particular grade attain clearly defined skills and knowledge for a specific Big6 stage.

The Super3™

As explained in the previous chapter, educators working with young students (pre–K to grade 2) may prefer to build their programs around the *Super3* (Plan—Do—Review) rather than the Big6.

The Super3 (see Figure 2.4) is the "pre-Big6" model of information problem-solving for very young children. The Super3 is a familiar, easy-to-remember, three-stage process for doing anything: a classroom task, an assignment, homework, a project, or even a fun activity. Like the Big6, the Super3 is widely applicable: to schoolwork, recreation, or decision making in kids' personal lives (e.g., what birthday present to get mom, what game to play with a friend).

Figure 2.5 repeats the Super3 by the Month schedule presented in Chapter 1. This schedule is modeled directly on the Big6 schedule displayed in Figure 2.3. We recommend spending two months on each of the Super3 stages. That will allow students to become very comfortable with the terminology and the actions to take for each stage.

Beginning the Big6 by the Month program with the Super3 for early grades is straightforward. Super3 stage 1 (Plan) matches Big6 stages 1 and 2 (Task Definition and Information Seeking Strategies). Super 3 stage 2 (Do) links to Big6 stages 3, 4, and 5 (Location & Access, Use of Information, Synthesis). Super3 stage 3 (Review) aligns with Big6 Stage 6 (Evaluation). See Figure 2.6 for the overall alignment and Figure 2.7 for a more detailed comparison.

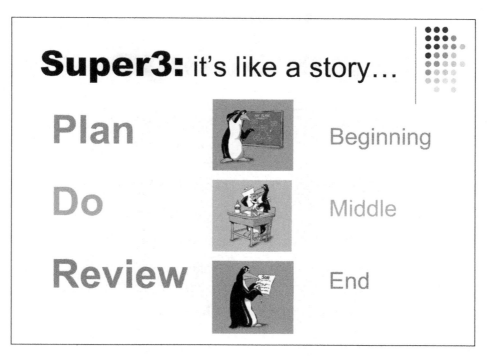

Figure 2.4 The Super3™

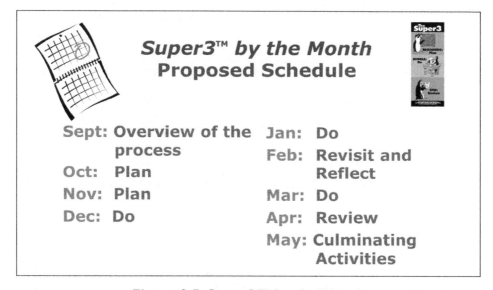

Figure 2.5 Super3™ by the Month

Alternatively, considering the attention spans and needs of young children, teachers may prefer shorter segments, cycling through the Super3 process twice during the school year. (See Figure 2.8.)

In future chapters, we present more detailed examples of plans articulated by month or grade level or both. Figure 2.9 is a sample of an annual plan for a specific grade—grade 4. Both the Super3 and Big6 are included to guide the month-to-month planning process for a range of student ability levels as well as to show how the two models work together seamlessly. The last column (CLASSROOM ASSIGNMENTS/UNITS) is provided for the curriculum connection, to document the subjects and assignments that will be used as the basis for Big6/Super3 learning.

To help you create your customized plan, we have provided an *Annual Grade Level Plan Template* (see the "Templates" section in the appendices).

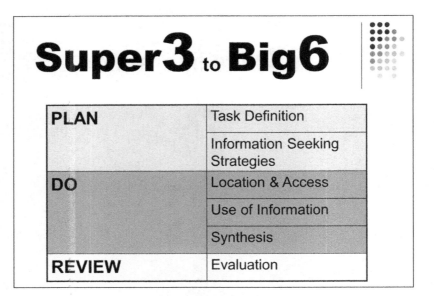

Super3 to Big6

PLAN	Task Definition
	Information Seeking Strategies
DO	Location & Access
	Use of Information
	Synthesis
REVIEW	Evaluation

Figure 2.6 Super3™—Big6™ Alignment

Super3™	Big6™

Plan
 	
• What am I supposed to do?
• What will it look like if I do a really good job?
• What do I need to find out to do the job?
	1. Task Definition
	  1.1 Define the information problem
	  1.2 Identify information needed (to solve the information problem)
	
	2. Information Seeking Strategies
	  2.1 Determine all possible sources (brainstorm)
	  2.2 Select the best sources

Figure 2.7 Super3™ to Big6™ Comparison

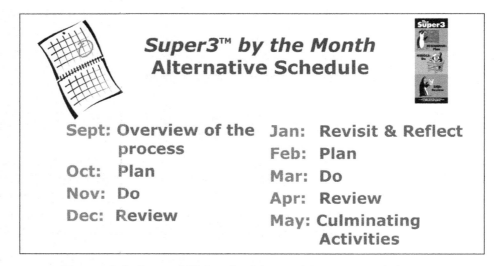

Super3™ by the Month
Alternative Schedule

Sept: Overview of the process
Oct: Plan
Nov: Do
Dec: Review

Jan: Revisit & Reflect
Feb: Plan
Mar: Do
Apr: Review
May: Culminating Activities

Figure 2.8 Super3™ by the Month Alternative Schedule

Grade: 4				
Month	AGENDA Super3™/Big6™	Big6™ Stage	GRADE LEVEL OBJECTIVES	CLASSROOM ASSIGNMENTS/UNITS
Sept	Overview: The Process		The Super3/Big6 process • in everyday life • in assignments	
Oct	PLAN Task Definition	1.1 1.2	Recognize tasks and assignments Select a topic from a list of choices	
Nov	PLAN Info Seeking Strategies	2.1 2.2	Choose from a range of resources Access libraries (print and online) to seek info for personal interest	
Dec	DO Location & Access	3.1 3.2	Use search engines (Google and article search)	
Jan	DO Use of Information	4.1 4.2	Extract facts from reading and media	
Feb	Revisit and Reflect			
Mar	DO Synthesis	5.1 5.2	Put facts in a logical order Use technology tools for presentation	
Apr	REVIEW Evaluation	6.1 6.2	Apply criteria Describe the process	
May	Culminating Activities/ Events		Complete a major subject area assignment	

Figure 2.9 Grade 4 Super3™/Big6™ by the Month Plan

Delivery-Centered versus Management-Centered Roles

The predictable approach offers a scalable plan to reach every student. This plan may seem like a daunting task, especially in large school districts with limited staff. How will you be able to reach all students? Mike distinguishes between *delivery-centered* and *management-centered* instructional roles for various educators: classroom teachers, teacher-librarians, technology teachers, and instructional coaches (see Figure 2.10).

"Delivery-centered" means that the role of the educator is to provide direct instruction through lessons or activities, working with the students in the classroom, library, computer lab, or elsewhere.

"Management-centered" refers to roles of planning, managing, and coaching—laying out the program, making the connections, working with other educators and administrators to ensure that all students are receiving ICT literacy instruction and learning the defined essential skills and knowledge.

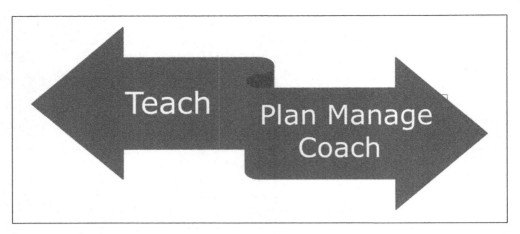

Figure 2.10 Delivery-Centered vs. Management-Centered Instruction

Figure 2.11 provides more detail about the responsibilities and actions of educators in delivery-centered versus management-centered contexts. In the next section, we offer a sample scenario of how roles are coordinated in a middle school setting.

Role	Delivery-Centered	Management-Centered
Teacher-Librarian **Technology Teacher**	• Teach lessons/mini-lessons to students. • Coordinate instruction with class-room assignments (and curriculum). • Assess student performance. • Report instruction and learning.	• Plan and manage instruction. • Provide lessons/mini-lessons to classroom teachers. • Coordinate assessment and reporting with classroom teachers. • Coach and advise classroom teachers. • Document and report instruction and learning.
Peer Coach	• Model and teach lessons/mini-lessons to students.	• Coach and advise all teachers on Big6 instruction and assessment. • Provide lessons/mini-lessons and assessment strategies. • Advise and coach on reporting.
Classroom Teacher	• Identify relevant content curriculum and assignments. • Teach lessons/mini-lessons to students. • Assess student performance. • Report student learning.	• Plan and manage learning for students. • Coordinate instruction with Teacher-Librarian, Technology Teacher, or others. • Determine and implement assessment and reporting approaches.

Mike Eisenberg, Big6 by the Month (2011).

Figure 2.11 Educator Roles in Different Contexts

Scenario

Consider this scenario for a middle school:

- Grades 6–8
- 900 total students, 300 per grade
- Each grade = 2 English, 2 social studies, 2 science, 2 math teachers (24 total)
- Teacher load = 5 classes per day × 30 students = 150
    - Core subject teachers organized in teams (2 teams per grade)
    - Other teachers: special education, health, music, art, languages (12 total)
    - 1 major assignment per class every 2 weeks (2 per month, 5 per quarter)
    - 1 teacher-librarian, 1 half-time clerical
    - .5 technology teacher

In this school of 900 students, it's not feasible for one educator (e.g., the teacher-librarian or technology teacher) to plan, manage, and deliver all the ICT literacy lessons. However, the teacher-librarian or the tech teacher (or ideally, both working together), adopting a management-centered approach, could plan and implement a comprehensive ICT literacy instructional program.

That's what happened in this school. The teacher-librarian and technology teacher worked with a small team of classroom teachers to:

- design the overall program—defining the two power learning objectives for each grade level per month;
- set and communicate the Big6 by the Month calendar;
- coordinate instructional lessons across subjects at each grade level so that every student received relevant lessons;
- develop and provide two Big6 lesson plans (linked to classroom assignments) per grade level per month;
- set assessment criteria and evidence; and
- coordinate reporting to students, faculty, parents, and administration.

The teacher-librarian and tech teacher also develop and teach lessons as needed and appropriate. The tech teacher is part-time, so she teaches 2–3 classes per day (10–15 per week; 40–60 per month) and the teacher-librarian is also able to handle a similar load (2–3 per day). The result is that students receive a minimum of four Big6, assignment-focused lessons each month to help them achieve the identified power learning objectives.

To help you design a plan for your school, we provide the *Program Plan Template*. In future chapters, we provide examples of how to use the plan to manage instruction and the overall program.

Lesson Ideas

The heart of the Big6 by the Month program is the lessons and instructional activities that the students engage in to learn the power learning objectives for that month. We target the specific, grade level power learning objectives for the Big6 stage or focus for that month, but always in the context of the overall Big6 process. We target specific lessons, activities, and assessments to the skill and learning objectives for that month.

This monthly focus is not meant to constrict or constrain. You can still develop and deliver a lesson or activity on a different Big6 skill in a given month if that's desired and appropriate. The monthly emphasis is on the main skill designated for that month (within the context of an assignment or curriculum topic), but the program is flexible enough to add additional instruction as needed.

Introducing the Super3™ or Big6™ Process to Students

In September, our overarching goal for the ICT literacy program is to introduce to or remind students that the Super3 or Big6 are *information problem-solving processes* that are useful whenever they have to make a decision or solve a problem that requires information.

We explain and emphasize that neither the Super3 nor Big6 is just a "school thing"; the Super3 and Big6 can be used for any information need: at home, school, work, or play. That's why we recommend introducing the Super3 or Big6 with an example from everyday life (see Figure 2.9). For example, "How would your family go about deciding what type of pet to acquire?" or "Where should your family go on vacation?" or "How would you and your friends select which movie to attend on Saturday?"

Using this last question as an example, we would first ask the students to consider what type of information they need to select a movie:

- their preferences (action vs. science fiction vs. romance, etc.)
- who they want to go with (and their preferences)
- the schedule (times it will be shown)
- age appropriateness and rating (Will it be okay with their parents?)
- quality ratings and reviews

We then discuss where and how the students will obtain the information they need (Big6 stage 2, Information Seeking Strategies). For example, possible sources are theater or movie websites, newspapers, talking to friends, personal knowledge (e.g., their schedules, likes and dislikes). We then move on to Location & Access, to find the specific information so that they can engage and extract what's relevant and credible (Use of Information). Synthesis in this case is primarily a decision: which movie, where, when, and with whom. After they've seen the movie, we can ask them to reflect on the entire process (Evaluation), asking how well the decision-making or problem-solving process worked and how they could improve it next time.

There are a number of lesson ideas and handouts on the Big6 website (http://www.big6.com/) related to teaching and learning the overall Super3 or Big6 process. See relevant links to "Banana Splits," "Super3 Dinosaur Lesson," "Sing a Song of Research," and others listed in the "Online Resources" section at the end of this chapter.

Measured

Assessment of student learning and the effectiveness of the overall ICT literacy program is vital for teachers and the school to know whether the program is successfully meeting its goals and objectives and to make adjustments and plan for the future. Students and their parents need to know whether or not they have achieved the desired ICT literacy goals and objectives.

We distinguish between *formative* and *summative* assessment. Kay Burke (2011) describes formative assessment as "assessment *for* learning": it occurs *during* the learning experience to provide ongoing feedback so that learning improves. Summative assessment is the traditional assessment *of* learning: the end-of-the-unit, end-of-the-quarter, end-of-the-course test, or final project that allows students to demonstrate what they have learned.

To select a monthly assessment approach, determine the specific skills, objectives, tools, and techniques to assess (see defined grade level objectives). Then select *evidence* to use for assessment (see Figure 2.12).

There are formal and informal, graded and ungraded types of evidence. You can collect evidence obtrusively, unobtrusively, and through student-generated means. With the evidence in mind, determine the *criteria* based on the learning objectives to clearly indicate the path to success (see Figure 2.13). Focus on student progress toward meeting objectives.

Samples of Evidence
Portfolios
Classroom assignments
Worksheets
Written work/reports
Lab reports
Observation checklists
Tests
Self-assessments
Video/audio reports
Contribution to discussion

Big6 by the Month: Task Definition (2011). Examples compiled by Colet Bartow.

Figure 2.12 Samples of Evidence

Examples of Criteria
Completeness
Frequency of display
Depth of understanding
Accuracy
Logic
Organization
Creativity/insight
Relevance
Credibility
Sources (number, type, range, quality)

Big6 by the Month: Task Definition (2011). Examples compiled by Colet Bartow.

Figure 2.13 Examples of Criteria

Use the language of summative assessment to help define levels of performance, such as the following:

- Novice
- Nearing Proficiency
- Proficient
- Advanced

TRAILS

Tool for Real-time Assessment of Information Literacy Skills

A Project of Kent State University Libraries

HOME

ABOUT TRAILS

HOW TRAILS WORKS

Steps to Using TRAILS

Ideas for Using TRAILS

Categories

MY ACCOUNT

FAQs

Related Resources

CONTACT US

Categories

1. Develop topic

Recognize need for information to address assignment. Develop questions to clarify and focus topic. Identify individuals and resources to help develop manageable topic based on the parameters of an assignment. Recognize the hierarchical relationships of broader and narrower topics to aid in revising the topic.

2. Identify potential sources

Understand information comes in various forms: textual, visual, audio, or data. Appreciate that each form offers differing types of information sources produced in a variety of formats (e.g., print or electronic books, film or streaming video). Understand the roles and limitations of differing types of information sources and the finding tools needed to access them (e.g., libraries, search engines, online catalogs). Select the most appropriate information sources and finding tools to address a given information need.

3. Develop, use, and revise search strategies

Create and revise search strategies. Understand how to use the features of an information source in order to retrieve the information needed (e.g., index and table of contents in a book, database filters). Develop a search strategy fitting for the given finding tool. Choose appropriate terms and keywords for searching a topic. Understand how to use search expanders and search limiters (e.g., logical operators) when too few, too many, or irrelevant results are returned.

4. Evaluate sources and information

Be able to determine the currency, relevance, authority, accuracy, and purpose of information or information sources. Recognize divergent perspectives. Recognize bias. Differentiate between fact and opinion.

5. Use information responsibly, ethically, and legally

Understand the concepts of intellectual property (especially copyright, fair use, and plagiarism) and of intellectual freedom. Understand how to cite and list sources using an appropriate style manual. Recognize how to take notes and paraphrase correctly.

TRAILS: Tool for Real-time Assessment of Information Literacy Skills
Copyright © 2016 Kent State University Libraries

Kent State University Libraries (2013). Categories. TRAILS: Tool for Real-time Assessment of Information Literacy Skills. http://www.trails-9.org/categories2.php?page=works

Figure 2.14 TRAILS Categories

Consistency is another key criterion for effectively measuring and describing how well students are able to apply the information problem-solving process. The language in a rubric should be specific to the grade level and easy for students and parents to understand.

One particularly valuable assessment tool that can be used in multiple grades is TRAILS: Tools for Real-Time Assessment of Information Literacy Skills, online tests developed at Kent State University (Kent State University Libraries, 2010, http://www.trails-9.org/). TRAILS uses multiple-choice questions to measure student achievement at grades 3, 6, 9, and 12. TRAILS questions are designed to assess five ICT skills, as noted in Figure 2.14.

These skills align directly with the Big6, although you can see that the Big6 encompasses much more than the TRAILS skills:

- Task Definition (1.1) contains "develop topic."
- Information Seeking Strategies (2.1) includes "identify potential sources" as well as "evaluate sources" (from TRAILS 4).
- Location & Access (3.1 and 3.2) requires students to "develop, use, and revise search strategies."
- Use of Information (4.1) includes "evaluate information."
- Synthesis (5.1 and 5.2) calls for "recogniz[ing] and "us[ing] information responsibly, ethically, and legally."

The TRAILS assessment site is free and includes capabilities for securely collecting and saving data on student performance. TRAILS assessments can be used as pre-tests, to provide formative feedback to students, or as summative post-tests.

We expand more on TRAILS and offer more depth on evidence and criteria and additional options for measurement in later chapters.

Reported

The final element of the Big6 by the Month Literacy Program is to develop and deliver at least two formal reporting mechanisms:

- Reporting on student achievement in relation to the defined power learning objectives.
- Reporting on the nature, scope, effectiveness, and efficiency of the ICT literacy program.

The student achievement reporting should be aimed at the students themselves as well as parents, teachers, and appropriate others. The program reporting communicates to the faculty, decision-making groups, building and district administration, and school board. See Figure 2.15 for the audiences and various reporting options.

Reporting methods will vary depending upon the audience, purpose, and approaches used in the school and district. For example, report cards in some schools already include a place for assigning a grade for technology or library skills. Other report cards allow for comments on subjects that are "taught, not graded" (e.g., physical education, music, art), and ICT literacy can be added to the report card.

If no existing mechanisms are currently available, we recommend compiling a monthly report to parents, administrators, and other teachers about the content and skills covered in that month, the activities students engaged in, and any assessment of student learning available. This could be attached to the report card or sent out separately (as well as posted online). Figure 2.16 is a sample short news report for parents that accompanied the second-quarter report card for students at Rossiter Elementary School in Helena, Montana. It briefly highlights and explains the Super3. Subsequent news reports can go into more depth or suggest ways for parents to help or encourage their children.

Audience	Options
Students	Exit tickets
Teachers	Grades on assignments
Administrators	Monthly/quarterly reports about student performance
Parents	Monthly/quarterly reports on the program
Public	Report card grades (on info and tech skills)
	Displays of student work

Figure 2.15 Reporting Audience and Options

News from the Library
Rossiter Elementary School
Second Quarter 2009–2010

SUPER3™: PLAN—DO—REVIEW

At Rossiter School, we begin learning about the **Super3** process at a young age. In fact, your child might have come home singing our "Plan, Do, and Review" song at some time! The **Super3** is a great framework for helping us do schoolwork, become better at something, or make decisions in our lives. You can even try it at home! It's simple:

Plan: Think about and decide what you need to do.

Do: Do it! Carry out your plan.

Review: Look back on what you did and think about whether you were successful and whether you should do something different next time.

In Library Skills classes, we especially use the Super3 process when we do research, but we try to keep it in mind for all of our activities.

Figure 2.16 Sample Newsletter

Summary

The purpose of the entire Big6 by the Month program is to ensure that students are able to thrive—today and in the future—in our informationally and technologically complex world. As explained, learning ICT literacy is too important for student success in all endeavors for it to be hit-or-miss, partial, or arbitrary. All students must have the opportunity to learn these essential skills and knowledge.

The Big6 by the Month approach takes the guesswork out of ICT literacy learning. It provides a conceptual and practical foundation and means to help you plan and deliver a comprehensive ICT literacy instructional program that is *defined* in terms of standards and grade level objectives, *predictable* in its implementation, *measured* according to established evidence and criteria, and *reported* in a variety of ways to a variety of audiences.

This chapter offered an overview of the entire program, along with descriptions and details on each of the four elements of the monthly program: defined, predictable, measured, and reported. Future chapters go into depth about these four elements and include planning worksheets, exercises to identify and match local learning standards with Common Core and other national and state efforts, sample schedules, lesson plans, assessment tools, and links to a rich set of Super3/Big6 curriculum and instructional resources.

The book can be used on its own, but it's also the companion piece for our nine-session webinar series, designed to provide monthly professional development for envisioning, planning, and implementing an ICT literacy program. The book and webinar series are intended to be useful to all educators: classroom teachers, teacher-librarians, technology teachers, and administrators. The list of recorded webinars is available in the appendices.

Online Resources

Useful Sites: Big6™

Big6 Associates, LLC, http://www.big6.com/

Big6 by the Month Google site, http://sites.google.com/site/big6xthemonth/home

Big6 by the Month discussion group, http://groups.google.com/group/b6month?hl=en

"The Big6 Skills Overview," http://big6.com/pages/about/big6-skills-overview.php

"Project Information Literacy, Information Overload, and the Big6," by Mike Eisenberg, http://big6.com/pages/lessons/articles/project-information-literacy.php

"Introducing the Big6" PowerPoint presentation, by Mike Eisenberg, http://big6.com/pages/lessons/presentations/introducing-the-big6.php

"Big6 Overview 2011" PowerPoint presentation, by Mike Eisenberg, http://big6.com/pages/lessons/presentations/big6-overview-2011.php

Big6 and Super3 overview handouts, http://big6.com/media/freestuff/Big6Handouts.pdf

"The Big6™ and Special Needs Students: My Personal Experience," by Laura Robinson, http://big6.com/pages/lessons/articles/the-big6trade-and-special-needs-students-my-personal-experience.php

"The Big6 Works: Empirical Evidence from One Middle School's Experience," by Dr. Emily S. Harris, http://big6.com/pages/lessons/articles/the-big6-works-empirical-evidence-from-one-middle-schoolrsquos-experience.php

"Sing a Song of Research: Turning the Big6 [and Super3] into a Tune," by Enid Davis, http://big6.com/pages/lessons/lessons/sing-a-song-of-research-turning-the-big6-into-a-tune.php

"Banana Splits," by Tammi Little, http://big6.com/pages/lessons/lessons/banana-splits.php

"'Plan, Do, Review . . . What's Bugging You?' (Grades PreK–2): An Information Literacy Lesson Plan for Young Children," by Theresa Benson, http://big6.com/pages/lessons/lessons/plan-do-reviewwhellipwhatrsquos-bugging-you-grades-prek-2-an-information-literacy-lesson-plan-for-young-children.php

"Super3 Dinosaur Lesson," http://big6.com/pages/lessons/lessons/super3-dinosaur-lesson.php

"Super3 Meets Flat Stanley!," by Sue Wurster, http://big6.com/pages/lessons/lessons/super3-meets-flat-stanley.php

"Super 3 for Kids!," by William P. Breitsprecher, http://www.slideshare.net/bogeybear/super-3-for-kids

Useful Sites: Standards

Common Core State Standards Initiative, http://corestandards.org/

Education World State Standards, http://www.educationworld.com/standards/

AASL Standards for the 21st Century Learner, http://www.ala.org/aasl/standards

Association of College and Research Libraries, "Information Literacy Competency Standards for Higher Education," http://www.ala.org/ala/mgrps/divs/acrl/standards/informationliteracycompetency.cfm

TRAILS: Tools for Real-Time Assessment of Information Literacy Skills, http://www.trails-9.org

ISTE National Educational Technology Standards (NETS) for Students, http://www.iste.org/standards

Essential Learning Expectations for Information Literacy (Montana), http://www.opi.mt.gov/pdf/Standards/10FebELE_LibMedia.xls

Partnership for 21st Century Skills, P21, *Learning for the 21st Century*, http://www.p21.org/index.php

"The Big6™ Helps Students Achieve Standards," by Janet Murray, http://big6.com/pages/lessons/articles/the-big6trade-helps-students-achieve-standards-by-janet-murray.php

"Big6™ Skills Aligned with Common Core Standards," http://janetsinfo.com/Big6_CCSSIStds.htm

"Big6™ Skills Aligned with ICT Literacy Standards," http://janetsinfo.com/Big6_ICTLitStds.htm

"Big6™ Skills Aligned with Texas Essential Knowledge and Skills (TEKS) Standards," http://janetsinfo.com/Big6_TEKSStds.htm

"Use the Internet with Big6™ Skills to Achieve Standards," by Janet Murray, http://janetsinfo.com/big6info.htm

"Big6 in Higher Education: Considering the ACRL Standards in a Big6 Context," by Ru Story-Huffman, http://big6.com/pages/lessons/articles/big6-in-higher-education-considering-the-acrl-standards-in-a-big6-context.php

Chapter 3

"WHO'S ON FIRST?"

October:
Task Definition

1.1 Define the information problem.
1.2 Identify information needed.

In This Chapter

- ❑ Introduction: Task Definition
- ❑ Defined: Standards and Grade Level Objectives
- ❑ Predictable: Lesson Ideas
- ❑ Measured: Assessment Criteria
- ❑ Reported: Report to Students and Parents
- ❑ Summary
- ❑ Online Resources

Introduction: Task Definition

In the Big6 by the Month program, you emphasize one particular Big6 (or Super3) skill stage per month, and in October the emphasis is on Task Definition. Task Definition is particularly crucial because it's pretty hard for students to be successful on an assignment or task if they don't fully grasp what's being asked of them.

In the early grades, Task Definition involves a range of actions—such as being able to follow directions, understand keywords in assignments, and choose a topic from a list of options. Task Definition also involves considering the information side of the assignment: how much information they need, what kinds of sources might be best (primary or secondary, factual or opinion), and what format is preferred (digital, print, graphic, video). As students advance in grades, they will hopefully assume more responsibility for their work (e.g., identifying essential questions that require answers, developing topic or thesis statements) and become more sophisticated in determining information requirements.

While our instructional focus in October is on Task Definition, we also continually remind students that Task Definition takes place in two key contexts: (1) the subject area, topic, unit, and assignment and (2) the overall Big6 (or Super3) information problem-solving process.

The Big6 information problem-solving model emphasizes that whenever students seek or apply information to solve a problem, complete an assignment, or make a decision, they (consciously or not) go through all Big6 stages. They don't necessarily complete these stages in a linear order, and a given stage doesn't have to take a lot of time and effort. However, to achieve success on an assignment or task, students must successfully complete all six stages.

To prepare for October's instruction and learning of Task Definition, we recommend that you develop objectives, plans, assessments, and reporting mechanisms using the four elements in the Big6 by the Month structure: Defined, Predictable, Measured, and Reported. Actions within each of these elements are explained below.

Defined

To begin planning a school- or district-wide emphasis on **Task Definition** for the month of October, we recommend first asking the following questions:

- Do students clearly understand their assignments?
- What types of information will they need in order to be successful?

Answers to these questions will help us *define* the Task Definition stage of the Big6 in terms of standards, grade level objectives, and *learning expectations*.

Standards for Task Definition

As noted previously, in addition to the Big6 website (www.big6.com) and Big6/Super3 books and materials, we rely on four main sources for explications of standards, objectives, and learning expectations for information and communication technology (ICT) literacy:

American Association of School Librarians, AASL. (2007). *AASL Standards for the 21st-Century Learner*. http://www.ala.org/aasl/standards

Association of College and Research Libraries, ACRL. (2008). "Information Literacy Competency Standards for Higher Education." http://www.ala.org/ala/mgrps/divs/acrl/standards/informationliteracycompetency.cfm

International Society for Technology in Education, ISTE. (2007). National Educational Technology Standards for Students (2nd ed.). http://www.iste.org/standards

Kent State University Libraries. (2010). TRAILS: Tools for Real-Time Assessment of Information Literacy Skills. http://www.trails-9.org/

The AASL and ACRL standards are based on conceptualizations and experiences of librarians over many years. Together, they cover pre-K through higher education and are very useful for identifying specific subskills under each of the Big6 stages. The ISTE NETS-S standards represent the best thinking of educators engaged with using technology for learning and teaching. TRAILS is an online information literacy assessment program that seeks to measure performance on information literacy items based on AASL and Common Core standards. These resources provide a rich base of ideas for identifying and defining the key power standards and learning objectives for each Big6 stage.

For the month of October, we want to focus on standards for Task Definition. Figure 3.1 identifies key standards from AASL, ACRL, TRAILS, and ISTE related to Task Definition, and Figure 3.2 does the same from the Common Core.

In Figure 3.1, notice the frequent references to an *inquiry process* and the repeated emphasis on asking *questions*. This is the essence of the Big6! The Big6 is an information problem-solving **process**: learning to ask good questions and find reliable answers is an essential skill for all of us, and one we need to help our students refine and develop. All research begins with a question; ultimately, our goal is to teach students to define their **own** tasks by asking good questions!

All teachers and students need to know that information literacy skills are important in all areas of the curriculum, not just as part of research. The Common Core State Standards Initiative (http://www.corestandards.org/the-standards)

ICT Literacy Standards Related to Task Definition	
AASL	1.1.3 Develop and refine a range of *questions* to frame the search for new understanding. 1.2.1 Display initiative and engagement by posing *questions* and investigating the answers beyond the collection of superficial facts.
ACRL	1.1 Defines and articulates the need for information.
TRAILS	1. Develop topic.
ISTE NETS-S	3a Plan strategies to guide *inquiry* 4a Identify and *define* authentic problems and *significant questions* for investigation

Compiled by Janet Murray from *AASL Standards for the 21st-Century Learner.* © 2007. American Association of School Librarians, http://www.ala.org/aasl/standards; "Information Literacy Competency Standards for Higher Education." © 2000. Association of College and Research Libraries, http://www.ala.org/ala/mgrps/divs/acrl /standards/informationliteracycompetency.cfm; TRAILS: Tools for Real-Time Assessment of Information Literacy Skills, http://www.trails-9.org/; and ISTE, National Educational Technology Standards (NETS-S) for Students. See "Big6™ Skills Aligned with ICT Literacy Standards," http://janetsinfo.com/Big6_ICTLitStds.htm.

Figure 3.1 ICT Literacy Standards Related to Task Definition

provides a national set of guidelines to describe what high school graduates must know and be able to do in order to succeed in entry-level college courses or the workplace. Some of these requirements pertain directly to identifying an information problem and planning a solution (see Figure 3.2).

Examine your state's content standards to find similar wording. (Use the *Standards Template*.)

Common Core Standards Related to Task Definition	
Writing	7. Conduct short as well as more sustained *research* projects based on *focused questions*, demonstrating understanding of the subject under investigation.

Mathematical Practices	1. Make sense of problems and persevere in solving them:
	  • *plan* a solution pathway
	4. Model with mathematics:
	  • apply mathematics to *solve problems* arising in everyday life

Compiled by Janet Murray and Colet Bartow from The Common Core State Standards Initiative, http://www.core standards.org/the-standards. See also "Big6™ Skills Aligned with Common Core Standards," http://janetsinfo.com /Big6_CCSSIStds.htm.

Figure 3.2 Common Core Standards Related to Task Definition

Grade Level Objectives

In preparing for October Task Definition instruction, we first review the standards and objectives from the above sources as well as state and local standards and then identify the priority "power" ICT literacy goals and learning objectives for all students in our school.

One important consideration is your school's capacity. That is, given your personnel situation and instructional time and effort available to devote to the ICT literacy program, how many power objectives can be addressed each month? We caution you not to try to do too much—especially the first time through the program. Try to start with two or four power objectives per grade level per month. Later you can build on this baseline, adjusting or adding objectives as you desire and are able. Remember: we are aiming for a comprehensive program with grade level objectives that will be attained by every student.

For example, Figure 3.3 displays Montana's *Essential Learning Expectations for Information Literacy* (http://www .opi.mt.gov/pdf/Standards/10FebELE_LibMedia.xls) related to Task Definition. Notice how many different skills are subsumed under the category "define the problem." Broad (italicized) objectives and skills that carry across all grades include

- task identification,
- topic selection,
- keywords, and
- setting a plan.

To help you plan and document the power learning objectives for each month and Big6 stage, we provide the *Grade Level Objectives Template* (see Figure 3.4) to create learning expectations for each grade level.

Cross-Grade Objective	Grade Level					
	K	1	2	3	4	5
5.1 BM 4 Use a variety of digital and print formats for pleasure and personal growth.	A. Identify personal interests.	A. Identify personal interests.	A. Identify personal interests.	A. Identify personal interests.	A. Identify personal interests.	A. Express personal interests.
1.1 Define the problem—*task identification.*	A. Listen and retell problem or task.	A. Listen and retell problem or task.	C. Recognize the problem or task.	C. Recognize the problem or task.	B. Restate the problem or task in their own words.	B. Summarize task.
1.1 Define the problem—*topic selection.*	C. Listen and retell the topic.	C. Listen and retell the topic.	A. Identify the topic.	A. Identify the topic.	A. Identify the topic.	C. Broaden or narrow topic.
1.1 Define the problem— *keywords.*	B. Retell keywords.	B. Retell keywords.	B. identify one or two keywords.	B. Recognize task-related vocab and keywords.	C. Use task-related vocab and keywords.	D. List keywords from topic.
1.1 Define the problem—*setting a plan* for information problem solving.	D. Listen to the steps needed to solve the problem or task.	D. Listen and retell the steps needed to solve the problem or task.	D. Retell the steps needed to solve the problem or task.	D. Discuss the steps needed to solve the problem or task.	D. Formulate questions or steps needed to solve the problem or task.	A. Formulate questions or steps needed to solve the problem or task.
1.2 Identify the *types and amount of information* needed.						1.1 E. List information requirements of the task.

Cross-Grade Objective	Grade Level				
	6	7	8	9–10	11–12
5.1 BM 8 Use and respond to a variety of print and digital formats for pleasure and personal growth.	A. Express areas of interest.	A. Express areas of interest.	A. Express and justify areas of interest.	A. Explore a variety of formats based on personal interest.	A. Explore a variety of formats based on personal interest.
1.1 Define the problem—problem or *task identification*.	B. Summarize task.	B. Summarize task.	B. Paraphrase task.	A. Develop a range of questions.	A. Develop and refine a range of questions.
1.1 Define the problem—*topic selection*.	C. Broaden or narrow topic.	C. Broaden or narrow topic.	C. Broaden or narrow topic.	D. Narrow or broaden the topic based on initial results.	C. Assess whether the problem is too narrow or broad and adjust accordingly.
1.1 Define the problem—*keywords*.	D. Identify keywords.	D. Identify keywords.	D. Identify or generate keywords. E. Confirm usefulness of keywords.	B. Formulate keywords. C. Validate usefulness of keywords.	B. Formulate and authenticate keywords within the problem.
1.1 Define the problem—*setting a plan* for information problem solving.	A. Formulate questions or steps needed to solve the problem or task.	A. Formulate questions or steps needed to solve the problem or task.	A. Formulate steps needed to solve the problem or task.		E. Appraise depth and complexity of problem.
1.2 Identify the *types and amount of information* needed.	1.1 E. List information requirements of the task.	1.1 E. List information requirements of the task.	1.1 F. Identify, list, and interpret information requirements of the task.	1.1 F. Assess need for more or less information.	

Compiled by Janet Murray from *Montana's Essential Learning Expectations for Information Literacy*, http://www.opi.mt.gov/pdf/Standards/10FebELE_LibMedia.xls.

Figure 3.3 Grade Level Objectives Related to Task Definition

		GRADES					
Grade Level Objectives	Cross-Grade Objective						

Figure 3.4 Grade Level Objectives Template

Since October is "Task Definition month," we can describe the activities to be accomplished using Big6/Task Definition terminology:

1.1 Define the information problem.

- Consult national standards, Common Core, and *your* state or district's content standards as background.
- Determine at least two to four power *Grade Level Objectives* per grade level for Task Definition.

1.2 Identify information needed.

- Determine capacity, based on personnel, curriculum, and school calendar.
- Review school-wide priorities and initiatives.
- Identify upcoming major assignments for each teacher and classroom in October.

With clear objectives identified and a sense of school-wide buy-in and available time and effort, we are ready to move on to the next element in the Big6 by the Month program: establishing a predictable instructional program for October that offers lessons and experiences for students to become more skilled in Task Definition.

Predictable

The Big6 by the Month Literacy Program is *predictable* on a number of levels; all those in the school community—teachers, administrators, parents, decision makers, and especially students—know the following:

- There is a specific Big6 or Super3 skill taught and learned each month.
- There are carefully selected and documented learning standards and objectives designated for each month's Big6 emphasis.
- Skills learning builds from month to month.
- Individual skills, tools, and techniques fit within the context of the overall Big6 or Super3 information problem-solving process.
- There is a progression in grade levels of sophistication and complexity of the skills taught and learned.

Delivering the specific instructional lessons and activities for this predictable program requires developing a monthly plan consistent with the school's calendar, organization, and schedule. Most important, the lessons and activities should fully integrate with classroom curriculum and assignments.

The easiest way to accomplish this is to identify one or two assignments for each teacher in each grade level, then develop Task Definition lessons targeted to classroom assignments or units.

Lesson Ideas for Super3™—PLAN

In situations using the Super3 with younger students, focus on PLAN, including helping students understand what an assignment asks them to accomplish and what sources they might use.

One successful PLAN lesson involves having students choose a format for creating a picture (see Figure 3.5). The overall assignment requires the students to make a picture of "Signs of Spring," but this lesson will work with almost any product-making assignment.

Super3™ Stage:	PLAN
Grade Level:	Pre-K, K
GL Objective:	Choose format for a picture (color/draw or cut/paste)
Subject Area:	Science
Unit Focus:	Signs of Spring

Figure 3.5 Early Elementary PLAN Lesson in Context

Subject Area Lesson Goal: Student(s) will recognize that there are different ways to make a picture, and they should be able to explain why they chose a certain format (draw/color or cut/paste pictures).

Learning Activity:

1. Give and explain the assignment to students.
2. Discuss what it means to "make a picture."
3. Have them brainstorm options.
4. Emphasize two choices: color/draw or cut/paste.
5. Discuss pros/cons for each.
6. Have each student choose a format and give one reason "why."

Assessment:

- Evidence: Student choice and explanation.
- Criteria: Able to choose and explain.

This instructional technique—presenting a task, discussing options, having students choose and explain why—is a simple way to help students learn to make Super3-related choices.

Lesson Ideas for Big6™—Task Definition

As explained above, Task Definition encompasses two substages:

1.1 Define the information problem

1.2 Identify information needed (to solve the information problem)

There is a range of actions, activities, and skills under each of these substages. For example, across all grades Big6 1.1, "Define the information problem," may include the following:

- Identify and understand keywords in assignments.
- Gain confidence with test instructions, structure, and format.
- Use graphic organizers.
- Engage in time management.
- Listen or read and then restate assignments/tasks in your own words.
- Choose from a list and justify "why."
- Break down an assignment into component parts.
- Use assignment or project organizers.
- Write a topic or thesis sentence or paragraph.

Big6 #1 Task Definition

Determine a purpose and need for information—What am I supposed to do?

What information do I need in order to do this? (Consider listing in question form.)
You will most likely find interesting additional information as you use the resources. List below information that you feel you need to know at this time.

1.

2.

http://library.sasaustin.org/assignmentOrganizer.php

Figure 3.6 Jansen's Sample Assignment Organizer

For Big6 substage 1.2, students need to identify *types* of information they will need to complete the task: facts, opinions, statistics, charts, tables, or graphs, pictures, or other forms of graphics. Students also need to consider information needs in terms of primary, secondary, and tertiary sources. Finally, students should be able to determine how much information they might need and how many sources they might want to use. In Task Definition 1.2, they focus on the attributes and nature of information and sources, not on selecting the specific sources themselves (as that takes place in Big6 stage 2, Information Seeking Strategies).

One way to make the assignment *predictable* is to present students with an *assignment organizer* and a *rubric* at the same time that you present the assignment. Barbara Jansen has created very effective assignment organizers based on the Big6 (see Figure 3.6). This sample assignment organizer guides students to rewrite the assignment in their own words and identify related questions that will help them explore the topic.

It can be helpful for students to identify the types of information they will need before they start their research. A graphic organizer (see Figure 3.7) can also help students organize and consider the types of information they will need; notice that both of these examples (above and below) are based on **questions.**

Several examples of Task Definition lessons in the context of classroom assignments follow.

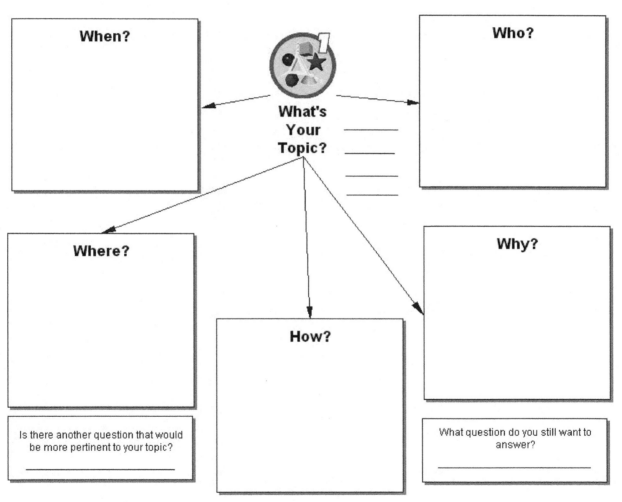

http://janetsinfo.com/TDgraphic.html

Figure 3.7 Graphic Organizer for Task Definition

Big6™ Stage:	Task Definition: 1.1 Define the problem.
Grade Level:	2–4
GL Objective:	Listen and retell the problem or task
Subject Area:	Science
Unit Focus:	Weather: Cloud Types

Figure 3.8 Elementary Level Task Definition (1.1) Lesson in Context

Subject Area Lesson Goal: Student(s) will create an illustration including labeled pictures of at least three different cloud types and one fact about each cloud type.

Example: Cirrus clouds are thin and wispy and are usually found at heights higher than 20,000 feet.

Learning Activity:

1. The whole class creates a KWHL (Know, Want to Know, How, Learn) chart related to cloud types. See Figure 3.9.

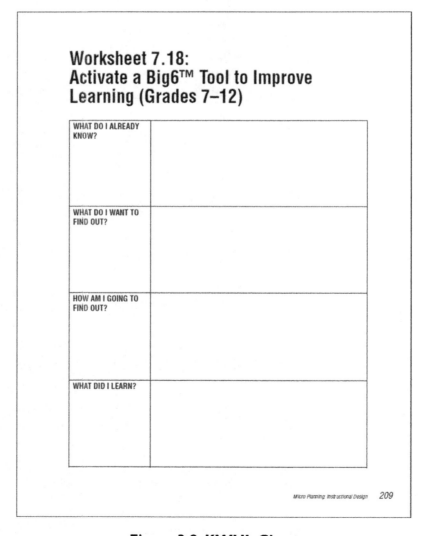

Figure 3.9 KWHL Chart

2. From the W part, the whole class generates a "Task Definition Statement" including:
   - the goal of the assignment,
   - the types of information needed, and
   - how students will complete the assignment.

Assessment:
   - Evidence: Responses of the whole class
   - Criteria: How easily the students complete the W part

Big6™ Stage:	Task Definition: 1.2 Identify the information needed
Grade Level:	4–6
Objectives:	Understand the nature (kinds, types) of information needed
Subject Area:	Social Studies
Unit Focus:	Regions of the United States

Figure 3.10 Elementary Level Task Definition (1.2) Lesson in Context

Subject Area Lesson Goal: Student(s) will work in small groups to research and create a presentation on one of the six regions of the United States (the Southwest, the Southeast, the Northeast, the Middle West, the Mountain States, the West). Each group must use at least four information sources.

Learning Activity: Each group creates a "bubble map" graphic organizer listing ALL the *types* of information they may possibly use.

Assessment:
   - Evidence: Bubble map
   - Criteria: Extent and completeness of bubble map

Big6™ Stage:	Task Definition: 1.1 Define the problem
Grade Level:	7–10
GL Objective:	Keywords—identify and define keywords in assignments
Subject Area:	Mathematics
Unit Focus:	Solving Story Problems

Figure 3.11 Secondary Level Task Definition (1.1) Lesson in Context

Subject Area Lesson Goal: Student(s) will use math computations to correctly solve math story problems.

Learning Activity:
   - Students will be given 8–10 story word problems.
   - Students will work with partners to read each problem and identify the keywords that tell what they must do.
   - Class will regroup and create a list of "keywords" for math story problems.

Assessment:

- Evidence: Quiz on keywords
- Criteria: Accuracy—aiming for 75% correct

Big6™ Stage:	Task Definition: 1.2 Identify the information needed
Grade Level:	11–12
GL Objective:	Types of information—recognize information requirements
Subject Area:	Literacy/Social Studies
Unit Focus:	Community

Figure 3.12 Secondary Level Task Definition (1.2) Lesson in Context

Subject Area Lesson Goal: Students are working on major, culminating "research" projects.

Learning Activity: The teacher discusses Big6 1.2—identifying the information needed:

- Discuss how Big6 1.2 differs from Big6 stage 2.1/2.2, which focuses on sources.
- Discuss how focusing on 1.2 can save time and effort *and* help them to get a better result/grade.

The class brainstorms items for a Big6 1.2 Checklist—e.g., amount of information, nature of the information (text, graphic, numerical), primary versus secondary sources. The class discusses the items and finalizes the checklist.

The class breaks into groups. Each group is to complete a checklist for four culminating assignment scenarios (provided by the teacher).

Assessment:

- Evidence: The four Big6 1.2 Checklists
- Criteria: Complete, insightful

To assist you in creating lessons in context, we provide the *Lesson Plan Template* in the appendices.

Measured

Comprehensive ICT literacy must include assessment and measurement of student performance. Assessment need not be arduous for students or burdensome for teachers. We simplify measurement by focusing on two aspects: evidence and criteria.

For *evidence*, we try to consider the forms of evidence and documentation available for determining student performance. Consider formal and informal, graded and ungraded types of evidence. You can collect evidence obtrusively, unobtrusively, or through student-generated means.

Criteria are the specific evaluation elements that can be applied to the evidence to determine student achievement in relation to stated learning objectives. Common criteria include degrees of completeness, accuracy, insightfulness, and frequency of display.

Performance descriptors are based on criteria. They encompass the range of student performance (e.g., novice to advanced) on selected criteria. For example, consider the language in Figure 3.13, a generalized, analytic performance description for eighth graders for Task Definition.

Sample Performance Descriptors for Task Definition: Grade 8			
Novice	*Nearing Proficiency*	*Proficient*	*Advanced*
Identify the topic incompletely and unclearly.	Identify the topic incompletely.	Identify the topic.	Identify and narrow in on the topic.
Recognize task-related vocabulary and keywords, demonstrating incomplete understanding.	Recognize some task-related vocabulary and keywords.	Recognize task-related vocabulary and keywords.	Make connections between task-related vocabulary and keywords.
Demonstrate a limited sense of the problem or task.	Omit important details of the problem or task.	Recognize the problem or task.	Relate the problem or task to past experiences.
Discuss the steps needed to solve the problem or task, omitting most steps.	Discuss the steps needed to solve the problem or task, omitting several steps.	Discuss the steps needed to solve the problem or task.	Discuss the steps needed to solve the problem or task with insightful dialogue.
Discuss and identify how many sources are needed.	Discuss and identify how many sources and one thing the sources should include (e.g., fact, opinions, graphics, chart).	Discuss and identify how many sources and two things the sources should include (e.g., fact, opinions, graphics, chart).	Discuss and identify how many sources and three or more things the sources should include (e.g., fact, opinions, graphics, chart).

Big6 by the Month: Task Definition (2011).

Figure 3.13 Sample Performance Descriptors for Task Definition

You can use the performance description to develop rubrics, checklists, or student self-evaluations to show where students' strengths and weaknesses in the problem-solving process may lie. The rubric should target specific skills to practice and measure in the context of content area knowledge.

With the Common Core State Standards, a rubric becomes particularly useful in helping to define what research (see Writing Standard 7) looks like at a particular grade level. You can break down "research skills" and then understand what types of support students need to successfully meet the expectation that they are doing research. The language in a rubric should be specific to the grade level and accessible to students and parents. Use the *Performance Descriptors Template* (see appendices) to distinguish among several levels of achievement.

In Figure 3.14, notice how this specific information literacy skill is addressed in the context of a science standard.

In Figure 3.15, a performance description has been added to the assessment plan from the Figure 3.11 example of a secondary level math lesson in context. Note that the vocabulary is age-appropriate and accessible to the student and clearly focused on each checkpoint along the performance continuum.

Science Grade 1 Example	
Content Standard: Montana Science Standard 1: Students, through the inquiry process, demonstrate the ability to design, conduct, evaluate, and communicate results and reasonable conclusions of scientific investigations.	B. Write a testable question with teacher guidance. E. Identify the purpose of the investigation.
Task Definition Focus: Approach	Students highlight question words and punctuation: model for class, group-generated questions, pair-generated questions. Students highlight lesson-specific vocabulary.
Sample Task Evidence and Criteria:	*Evidence:* Student written or dictated question(s) using appropriate question words and vocabulary. Checklist *Criteria*: 1. Accuracy: correct question words/ punctuation/vocabulary highlighted. 2. Completion: all question words/punctuation/ vocabulary underlined.

Big6 by the Month: Task Definition (2011). Developed by Colet Bartow.

Figure 3.14 Science Grade 1 Assessment Example

Big6™ Stage:	*Task Definition: 1.1 Define the problem*
Grade Level:	7–10
GL Objective:	Keywords—identify and define keywords in assignments
Subject Area:	Mathematics
Unit Focus:	Solving Story Problems

Figure 3.15 Performance Description for Secondary Task Definition (1.1) Lesson

Subject Area Lesson Goal: Student(s) will use math computations to correctly solve math story problems.

Learning Activity:

- Students will be given 8–10 story word problems.
- Students will work with partners to read each problem and identify the keywords that tell what they must do.
- Class will regroup and create a list of "keywords" for math story problems.
- EXTENSION: Students will use their knowledge of mathematics to define each keyword.

Assessment:

- Evidence: Quiz on keywords.
- Criteria: Accuracy—aiming for 75% correct.

Novice	Nearing Proficient	Proficient	Advanced
Recognize task-related vocabulary and keywords, demonstrating incomplete understanding.	Recognize some task-related vocabulary and keywords.	Recognize task-related vocabulary and keywords.	Make connections between task-related vocabulary and keywords.

Big6 by the Month: Task Definition (2011). Developed by Colet Bartow.

Reported

If your ICT literacy program is clearly defined, predictably delivered, and measured, you are well on your way to helping students gain these essential skills and knowledge. But it's also crucial to share information about the program and student progress with the students themselves, parents, and other teachers and administrators in the school and district.

Reporting can be time-consuming and tedious, so we need to think about highly effective ways to report student advancement. One option is to include ICT literacy on traditional report cards, but we also want to inform students and parents, as well as other teachers, about how well a student knows and is able to do what we have defined through content and information literacy standards.

Reporting methods will vary depending on the audience. For example, "Exit Tickets" at the end of a lesson (see Figure 3.16) ask students to pause and consider what they have learned. They may include a cue such as "Today in science I learned:" or ask students to list a question they still want answered.

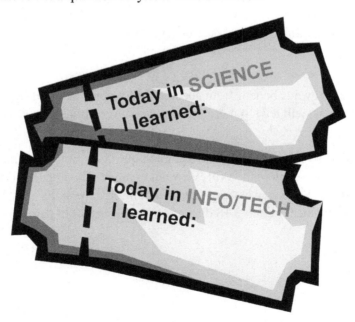

Figure 3.16 Sample Exit Ticket

My Project	My Ideas	
What is the topic of this assignment/project?		
What are some of the keywords you have learned that relate to the topic? List five (5) vocabulary words and three (3) keywords.	1. 2. 3. 4. 5.	1. 2. 3.
What is the big question you are trying to answer about this project? What are some of the things you wonder about the topic?		
What is your plan for answering this big question?		
What sources are you thinking about using? List at least three (3) types of sources. Why do you think those are the best sources to use?		

Big6 by the Month: Task Definition (2012). Developed by Colet Bartow.

Figure 3.17 Student Planning Sheet for Task Definition

Report to Students

Students can use the "plan" in Figure 3.17 to discuss their work with parents, classmates, or other teachers. This planning sheet becomes part of the evidence of learning for a project, and completeness can be the criterion for success if the planning sheet is a graded part of the project. When matched with the report to parents, we can further support meaningful conversations about learning between parents and students.

Report to Parents

Parents and caregivers can always benefit from specific information that will help them help their students succeed. Sometimes a list of questions will lead to more productive conversations related to what students are expected to know and be able to do.

Because Task Definition is so focused on how to ask good questions, it is only fair that we share good questions with parents that will enable them to explore the skills we want to target. The important thing is to encourage conversation between parents and students. Such conversations serve to reinforce the skills of task definition and allow students to share their learning with confidence. Figure 3.18 displays a sample report to parents.

Sample Message for October:	Students will be able to:	Questions to ask:
Dear Parents/Guardians: During the month of October, your student will work on a variety of projects and assignments. As part of each project, we will focus on Stage 1 of the Big6 information problem-solving model. You can help reinforce these skills by asking your student questions that relate to: 1.1 *Defining* the topic and problem to be solved 1.2 *Identifying* information needed to solve the problem. The chart in this message details the skills students will practice and some questions you can ask to help students be successful as they complete assignments and projects. Please contact me if you have any questions. [insert contact information]	Identify the topic.	What is the topic of this assignment/project?
	Recognize task-related vocabulary and keywords.	What are some of the key-words you have learned that relate to the topic?
	Recognize the problem or task.	What is the big question you are trying to answer about this project? What are some of the things you wonder about the topic?
	Discuss the steps needed to solve the problem or task.	What is your plan for answering this big question?
	Discuss and identify how many sources they will need and two things the sources should include (e.g., fact, opinion, graphics, chart).	What sources are you thinking about using? Why do you think those are the best sources to use?

Big6 by the Month: Task Definition (2012). Developed by Colet Bartow.

Figure 3.18 Sample Report to Parents, Task Definition

Summary

The comprehensive Big6 by the Month program zeros in on Task Definition in the month of October.

We first carefully *define* the Task Definition, grade level appropriate power objectives, by consulting various ICT literacy standards and content standards (e.g., the Common Core State Standards) related to the inquiry process. The Big6 by the Month program emphasizes quality over quantity—not simply creating another laundry list of dozens of standards and objectives that will never be addressed with students. Rather, we compile a highly selected set of two to four essential Task Definition power objectives per grade and commit to providing instruction and learning opportunities for every student to attain these objectives.

The October program is *predictable*. Every student, teacher, parent, and member of the school community knows that October is Task Definition month, and students will be developing their Super3 PLAN or Big6 Task Definition skills and knowledge in conjunction with classroom curriculum and assignments. Teacher-librarians, classroom teachers, and technology teachers create lesson plans for local content assignments that emphasize each of the grade level objectives. One way to make assignments predictable is by using an assignment organizer and a consistent format.

As with all important curriculum areas, learning must be *measured* and assessed. In the Big6 by the Month program, we do so by clearly identifying the evidence and criteria as well as the performance descriptors by which students will be assessed.

Finally, each month we *report* widely about the program and student progress. Report cards, monthly newsletters or reports, websites, and meetings are just a few of the ways to engage students, as well as their teachers, parents, and administrators in the ICT literacy program.

Online Resources

Useful Sites: Task Definition

"Big6™ Writing Process Organizer," by Barbara Jansen, http://big6.com/pages/lessons/lessons/big6-writing
-process-organizer.php

"Big6 Assignment Organizer for Grades 7–12," by Barbara Jansen, http://library.sasaustin.org/assignment
Organizer.php

"How to Get an 'A'," by Melanie Bonanza and Sara Schepis, http://big6.com/pages/lessons/lessons/how-to-get
-an-a.php

"Critical Thinking, Task Definition and the Reference Interview," by Ru Story-Huffman, http://big6.com/pages
/lessons/articles/critical-thinking-task-definition-and-the-reference-interview.php

"The Big6 Task Definition Tools in Higher Education," by Ru Story-Huffman, http://big6.com/pages/lessons
/articles/big6-task-definition-tools-in-higher-education.php

Big6 Breaking Down Your Assignment (YouTube video grades 7–9) http://www.youtube.com/user/Big6Skills#p
/a/u/2/l5x7pdsjgmY

"Activate a Big6 Tool to Improve Learning" (Grades 7–12), by Bob Berkowitz, http://big6.com/pages/lessons
/lessons/kwhl-chart.php

"What's Your Topic?" Task Definition Graphic Organizer, by Janet Murray, http://janetsinfo.com/TDgraphic.html

Graphic Organizers, http://www.graphic.org/goindex.html

"Ask Essential Questions," by Janet Murray, http://janetsinfo.com/ask.htm

TRAILS Information Literacy Lesson Plans, http://trails-informationliteracy.wikispaces.com/Lesson+Plans

Chapter 4

"ISN'T IT ALL ON THE INTERNET ANYWAY?"

November:
Information Seeking Strategies

2.1 Determine all possible sources.

2.2 Select the best sources.

In This Chapter

❏ Introduction: Information Seeking Strategies

❏ Defined: Standards and Grade Level Objectives

❏ Predictable: Lesson Ideas

❏ Measured: Performance Descriptors

❏ Reported: Report to Students and Parents

❏ Summary

❏ Online Resources

Introduction: Information Seeking Strategies

No, "it's not all on the Internet," and in November we help students to learn about the wide (and changing) range of information sources, as well as how to find information that is *relevant* to different information needs and that is *credible* in terms of authority, reliability, validity, currency, bias, and other dimensions. Relevance and credibility are the two major concepts about which students will develop increasing depths of understanding and sophistication each year.

Instruction in information seeking strategies is a long-standing, baseline component of information literacy instruction. While the specific sources, tools, and systems have changed due to technology, concepts such as relevance and credibility are enduring. That's why Information Seeking Strategies includes two important substages, one that identifies *all* possible sources and another that involves determining the *best* sources within the contexts and constraints of the task, problem, or question at hand:

Information Seeking Strategies

    2.1 Determine all possible sources (brainstorm)

    2.2 Select the best sources

Young students—even if they can't read or write—can think about what sources they might use to answer questions or find out something. They can brainstorm individually, in groups, or as a class. They can tell you "why" they might use a particular source, for example, "my Mom knows everything" or "there's lots of stuff on YouTube" or "I just like picture books." Older students will (hopefully) refer to relevance and credibility and identify subconcepts such as "on the topic," "from a well-known person," "up-to-date," or "easy to use."

The following sections outline and describe how to plan and implement practical and doable Information Seeking Strategies instruction and learning in November to meet the needs of all students in your school.

Defined

Today's students tend to rely almost exclusively on Google searches to seek information. Do they also consider books in the library? Online article databases? People to interview? How do they decide which sources are "best?" We want students to be expert Google searchers (and we'll focus instruction on Boolean logic, commands, and search tips and techniques next month as part of Location & Access). Here, we want students to recognize the wide scope of information sources and be able to determine the best sources to match a particular task.

As explained earlier, to select the key, specific understandings and skills for students to learn under each Big6 or Super3 stage, the Big6 by the Month program *defines* each stage of the Big6 in terms of standards augmented by grade level objectives or learning expectations.

Standards for Information Seeking Strategies

All of the sources of information and communication technology (ICT) literacy standards emphasize the importance of considering a *variety* of sources of information and *evaluating* sources and their content (see Figure 4.1). AASL, for example, refers to "find, evaluate, and select appropriate sources." These are really three distinct actions—find, evaluate, and select—and we caution against combining them in a single standards or objectives statement. We prefer the approach of ACRL (and others) to separate the acts of identifying a variety of sources and evaluating information and sources.

In the Common Core State Standards, we see how ICT literacy skills are central to all areas of the curriculum. Those pertaining directly to Information Seeking Strategies (see Figure 4.2) include "gather relevant information from multiple print and digital sources" and "assess the credibility and accuracy of each source." These are standards that relate to Big6 stage 2, Information Seeking Strategies and to Big6 stage 4, Use of Information.

For example, under Reading, "Trace and evaluate the argument and specific claims of a text" involves assessing sources for relevance and credibility—which are part of Information Seeking Strategies. However, tracing and evaluating arguments and claims of a text are also part of the Use of Information actions of engaging information. Critiquing the reasoning of others (in the Mathematical Practices category) is similarly Use of Information. Information problem-solving is a process, and a particular standard or skill is sometimes applied at more than one point in time.

Ultimately, your task is to identify and select the important, specific Information Seeking Strategies learning objectives for November. As in other months, we recommend that you examine local and state content standards for wording similar to CCSS as well as to identify additional objectives for Information Seeking Strategies. Then, use the *Standards Template* to document and expand on your choices.

ICT Literacy Standards Related to Information Seeking Strategies	
AASL	1.1.4 Find, *evaluate*, and select appropriate sources to answer questions.
	1.1.5 *Evaluate* information found in selected sources on the basis of accuracy, validity, appropriateness for needs, importance, and social and cultural context.
ACRL	1.2 Identifies a *variety* of types and formats of potential sources for information.
	3.2 Articulates and applies initial criteria for *evaluating* both the information and its sources.
TRAILS	2. Identify potential sources.
	4. *Evaluate* sources and information.
ISTE NETS	3c. *Evaluate* and select information sources and digital tools based on the appropriateness to specific tasks.

Compiled by Janet Murray from *AASL Standards for the 21st-Century Learner* © 2007, American Association of School Librarians, http://www.ala.org/aasl/standards; "Information Literacy Competency Standards for Higher Education" © 2000, Association of College and Research Libraries, http://www.ala.org/ala/mgrps/divs/acrl/standards/informationliteracycompetency.cfm; TRAILS: Tools for Real-Time Assessment of Information Literacy Skills, http://www.trails-9.org/; and ISTE, National Educational Technology Standards (NETS-S) for Students. See "Big6™ Skills Aligned with ICT Literacy Standards," http://janetsinfo.com /Big6_ICTLitStds.htm.

Figure 4.1 ICT Literacy Standards Related to Information Seeking Strategies

Common Core Standards Related to Information Seeking Strategies	
Reading: Informational Text	8. Trace and *evaluate* the argument and specific claims in a text, distinguishing claims that are supported by reasons and evidence from claims that are not.
Reading: History and Social Studies	6. Identify aspects of a text that reveal an author's *point of view* or purpose (e.g., loaded language, inclusion or avoidance of particular facts).
	8. Distinguish among *fact, opinion*, and *reasoned judgment* in a text.
Writing	8. Gather relevant information from multiple print and digital sources, assess the *credibility* and *accuracy* of each source....
Mathematical Practices	3. Construct viable arguments and *critique* the *reasoning* of others: ... distinguish correct logic or reasoning from that which is flawed.

Compiled by Janet Murray and Colet Bartow from The Common Core State Standards Initiative, http://www.corestandards.org /the-standards. See also "Big6™ Skills Aligned with Common Core Standards," http://janetsinfo.com/Big6_CCSSIStds.htm.

Figure 4.2 Common Core Standards Related to Information Seeking Strategies

Grade Level Objectives

Figure 4.3 shows an example of Information Seeking Strategies objectives based on the national standards documents noted above as well as the state of Montana's *Essential Learning Expectations for Information Literacy* (http://www.opi.mt.gov/pdf/Standards/10FebELE_LibMedia.xls). Notice how many different skills can be subsumed under the category "evaluate and select appropriate sources":

- Consider a range of resources.
- Evaluate in terms of currency, point of view, and usefulness.

Cross-Grade Objective	Grades					
	K	1	2	3	4	5
1.2 Determine the resources needed.	A. Explore possible resources.#	A. Discuss possible resources.#	A. Discuss possible resources.#	A. Discuss and identify possible resources.#	A. Construct a list of possible resources.*	A. List possible resources.*
1.3 Choose from a *range of resources*.	A. Explore possible resources.#	A. Choose resources from a limited selection.	A. Choose resources from a limited selection.	A. Determine relevant resources.	A. Construct a list of possible resources.*	
1.3 BM 8 *Evaluate* and select appropriate resources: *currency*.						A. Identify the copyright date to determine the currency of resources.
1.3 BM 8 *Evaluate* and select appropriate resources: *point of view*.						B. Identify point of view in resources.
1.3 BM 8 *Evaluate* and select appropriate resources: *usefulness*.						C. Identify and select useful resources.

Cross-Grade Objective	Grades				
	6	7	8	9–10	11–12
1.3 BM 8 *Evaluate* and select appropriate resources: *currency*.	A. Determine the currency of resources.	A. Identify appropriately current resources.	A. Identify appropriately current resources.		
1.3 BM 8 *Evaluate* and select appropriate resources: *point of view*.	B. Identify point of view in resources.	B. Identify point of view and bias in resources.	B. Identify point of view and bias in resources.		

Cross-Grade Objective	Grades				
	6	7	8	9–10	11–12
1.3 BM 8 *Evaluate* and select appropriate resources: *usefulness.*	C. Judge authority and usefulness of resources.	C. Appraise authority and usefulness of resources.	C. Appraise validity, authority, and usefulness of resources.		
1.3 D *Select the best resources.*	D. Select the best resources.	D. Select the best resources.	D. Select the best resources.	A. Identify accurate information (RADCAB[**]).	A. Interpret information for RADCAB.[**]
1.3 BM 12 Evaluate and select appropriate resources.				B. Evaluate all selected topic-related resources based on task criteria.	B. Compare and contrast all selected topic-related resources based on task criteria.
1.3 BM 12 Evaluate and select appropriate resources.				C. Distinguish between and incorporate appropriate primary/ secondary sources.	C. Incorporate primary and/ or secondary sources appropriately.

Compiled by Janet Murray from Montana's *Essential Learning Expectations for Information Literacy*, http://www.opi.mt.gov/pdf/Standards/10FebELE_LibMedia.xls.

BM = benchmark

[#]print, nonprint, digital, community resources

[*]for example, reference materials, newspapers, age-appropriate websites, nonfiction books, personal interviews, audio files, video files, community resources, databases

[**]RADCAB = Relevance, Appropriateness, Detail, Currency, Authority, Bias

Figure 4.3 Grade Level Objectives Related to Information Seeking Strategies

Grade level objectives related to evaluating sources might expect students to consider the relevance, authority, validity, currency, and objectivity of the sources they select to use for research. Use the *Grade Level Objectives Template* to create learning expectations for each grade level at your school.

Predictable

By November, your Big6 by the Month program should begin to be recognized as being *predictable* to a particular Big6 or Super3 stage. Reflect on October's program in terms of capacity and what seems to be possible to accomplish in a month. As always, we strive to place ICT literacy instruction in two contexts: the overall Big6 (or Super3) process and the classroom curriculum. We connect to the classroom by identifying one or two assignments for each grade and teacher. We then develop Information Seeking Strategies lessons targeted to classroom assignments or units.

Lesson Ideas for Super3™—PLAN

Last month, we included a Super3 lesson for PLAN using the "Signs of Spring" unit and picture-making assignment. We worked with the young students on recognizing their task (making a picture), choosing from options they have for creating the picture (color/draw or cut/paste), and explaining why.

Here, in November, we continue to work on Super3 stage PLAN, but now we focus on planning related to getting the information young students need to accomplish a task. This parallels Big6 stage 2—Information Seeking Strategies—because everyone needs to plan two things: what you are supposed to do and what information you need to do it. Even young children can recognize that they need to figure out the task and the information.

In situations using the Super3 with younger students, focus on PLAN; help students understand what an assignment asks them to accomplish and what sources they might use.

Figure 4.4 outlines a simple lesson building on the same "Signs of Spring" assignment, and Figure 4.5 presents a lesson in the form of a game: making the connections among task, information, and sources.

Super3™ Stage:	PLAN
Grade Level:	Pre-K, K
GL Objective:	Choose from two possible sources
Subject Area:	Science
Unit Focus:	Signs of Spring

Figure 4.4 Early Elementary PLAN (Sources) Lesson in Context

Subject Area Lesson Goal: Student(s) will recognize that they have choices in terms of information sources. We have them brainstorm many sources but then narrow to just two types: books (found in the library, classroom, or home) or people (Mom, Dad, siblings, teacher, librarian, friends). The lesson requires them to consider the two choices, to select one, and to explain why they chose that source.

Learning Activity:

1. Remind the students of the assignment.
2. Discuss what information they need and why.
3. Have them brainstorm options for sources.
4. Guide the discussion to two types of sources: books and people.
5. Discuss pros/cons for each.
6. Have each student choose a source and provide one reason "why."

Assessment:

- Evidence: Student choice and explanation.
- Criteria: Able to choose and explain.

This lesson uses the same instructional technique as last month: presenting a task, discussing options, having students choose and explain why. This is an easy way to help students begin to make Super3, information-related choices.

The next lesson builds on previous Super3 PLAN lessons. Students should have had previous instruction on understanding tasks and problems as well as choosing good sources. Here, we put it all together: making the connections from task to information to sources.

Super3™ Stage:	PLAN
Grade Level:	K, 1, 2
GL Objective:	Identify information sources for various tasks
Subject Area:	All
Unit Focus:	Problem Solving

Figure 4.5 Early Elementary PLAN (Game) Lesson in Context

Subject Area Lesson Goal: Students will recognize the connections among *task*, *information needed*, and *sources*. For example, if given a task to learn about birds, they will realize that they need facts and some pictures and that they can get facts and pictures from the web, from books, and by observation.

Learning Activity:

1. Tell the class we are going to play the Super3 PLAN game.

2. Create teams of three. Each team will get a chance to answer twice.

3. The students will be presented with a task, and they need to identify (1) two information items they would want to find out about for the task and (2) two sources that would have that information.

4. A team can earn four points each round: two points for each information item and two points for each source.

5. Use a chart on the whiteboard, screen, or smartboard to keep track (see Figure 4.6 for a partially completed sample chart).

Group	Task	Information	Sources
Red	Learn about birds	Facts—different kinds, where they live. Pictures.	Books, web, observation.
Purple	Win soccer game	Good players on the other team. Our strategy.	Friends, myself, coach, observation.
Orange	Math homework	Questions. How to do it.	Teacher, handout, myself.
…	…	…	…

Figure 4.6 Super3™ PLAN Chart

Assessment:

- Evidence: Group performance. Participation in group decisions.
- Criteria: Accurate. Appropriate. Realistic.

There are many variations to this Super3 PLAN game, and it can be a regular activity (e.g., once a month) for a class. Over time, the students should get better and better at linking Task—Information—Sources. We can also create a similar game for Big6 stages 1 and 2, Task Definition and Information Seeking Strategies.

Lesson Ideas for Information Seeking Strategies

Big6 2.0 Information Seeking Strategies

2.1 Determine all possible sources (brainstorm)

2.2 Select the best sources

Information Seeking Strategies has two clear actions: first, to be able to identify the widest possible range of sources, and second, to select the best sources for a particular need, problem, or task. To students, we emphasize "all" and "best" when they learn about information sources and systems.

Consider *all* possible resources (available, affordable, grade level appropriate, etc.).

Select the *best* sources; as we have seen in the grade level objectives above, students need to consider several elements to identify and qualify the best sources:

- Reliable (Is the information true?)
- Authoritative (Who's the author?)
- Current (Date of update? Does it matter?)
- Objectivity (Point of view, opinion, bias)
- Relevance (Appropriateness to topic)

Several examples of Information Seeking Strategies lessons in the context of classroom assignments are shown in the figures below.

Big6™ Stage:	Information Seeking Strategies: 2.1 Determine all possible sources
Grade Level:	Second Grade
GL Objective:	Determine the resources needed
Subject Area:	Science
Unit Focus:	Simple Machines

Figure 4.7 Elementary Information Seeking Strategies (2.1) Lesson in Context

Subject Area Lesson Goal: Students will create a labeled diagram of a simple machine (lever, inclined plane, pulley) and will write one paragraph to describe how the machine has helped in their lives.

Learning Activity:

1. The whole class will create Post-it® notes of all possible sources to use for this assignment.
2. The Post-its will be grouped by type (print, nonprint, digital, people).
3. The groupings will be displayed in the classroom, and students may add details to the Post-it notes throughout the duration of the assignment.

Assessment:

- Evidence: Post-it notes displayed in the classroom.
- Criteria: Each child contributes at least three possible source ideas (Post-it notes).

Novice	Nearing Proficient	Proficient	Advanced
A. Identifies random resources from a limited selection.	A. Identifies a minimal number of resources from a limited selection.	A. Identifies resources from a limited selection.	A. Identifies relevant resources from a limited selection.

Big6 by the Month: Information Seeking Strategies (2010). Developed by Laura Robinson. Assessment by Colet Bartow (2011).

Big6 Stage:	Information Seeking Strategies: 2.2 Select the best sources
Grade Level:	Grades 9/10
GL Objective:	1.3 BM 12 Evaluate and select appropriate resources
Subject Area:	World History
Unit Focus:	World War I and World War II

Figure 4.8 Secondary Information Seeking Strategies (2.2) Lesson in Context

Subject Area Lesson Goal: Students will compose five to seven journal entries (one page each) from the perspective of people who lived during World War I or World War II and will discuss how technology or practices (poison gas, trench warfare, machine guns, airplanes, submarines, and tanks) affected them. See Figure 4.8.

Learning Activity:

1. Students will work in groups to create a list of *all* possible sources (print, nonprint, digital, community) to help with their assignment.

2. Students will work individually to select at least three sources to use for their assignment and will explain (in two or three sentences) *why* they chose that particular source, focusing on relevance and credibility.

Assessment:

- Evidence: Individuals select at least three sources.
- Criteria: At least three sources (two different types) are selected AND the students explain why (logically and accurately) they selected the sources (e.g., topical, current, trustworthy, precise, etc.).

Novice	Nearing Proficient	Proficient	Advanced
E. Selects minimal relevant resources without explanation.	E. Selects some resources to solve the problem with incomplete explanation.	E. Selects and justifies appropriate resources to solve the problem.	E. Selects and justifies unique resources to solve the problem.

Big6 by the Month: Information Seeking Strategies (2010). Developed by Laura Robinson. Assessment by Colet Bartow (2011).

A reminder: We have provided the *Lesson Plan Template* to develop consistency in lessons. (See appendices or the electronic version at https://sites.google.com/site/big6xthemonth/file-cabinet.)

Measured

In the Big6 by the Month program, we operationalize measurement and assessment by looking for evidence of student performance and then applying clear criteria related to the Big6 stage. In this month, we want to be able to determine how well students are able to engage in the actions of Information Seeking Strategies—that is, identifying and evaluating a wide range of types and specific sources. Here are some examples:

- In workshops, Mike Eisenberg suggests that students don't simply include a bibliography with their final work but rather annotate the bibliography, indicating *why* they selected each source and what makes it the best one for this particular assignment.

- Assess students' ability to evaluate Internet resources by introducing them to bogus or "hoax" websites, then asking pointed questions about the information displayed on the site.

- Use the TRAILS (http://www.trails-9.org) site to evaluate students' information literacy skills.

Novice	Nearing Proficient	Proficient	Advanced
Struggle to identify information as accurate.	Sometimes identify information as accurate.	Identify accurate information.	Discriminate the accuracy of information.
Evaluate few topic-related resources.	Evaluate some topic-related resources based on task criteria.	Evaluate all topic-related resources based on task criteria.	Determine the applicability of all topic-related resources to the task criteria.
Distinguish between and rarely incorporate both primary and secondary sources.	Distinguish between and sometimes incorporate appropriate primary/ secondary sources.	Distinguish between and incorporate appropriate primary/secondary sources.	Creatively incorporate appropriate primary/ secondary sources.
Reevaluate the problems and resources; refine with limited success.	Sometimes reevaluate the problems and resources; refine if needed.	Reevaluate the problems and resources; refine if needed.	Reevaluate the problem and appropriate resources; refine proactively.
Select minimal relevant resources.	Select some resources to solve the problem.	Select appropriate resources to solve the problem.	Select unique resources to solve the problem.

Big6 by the Month: Information Seeking Strategies (2011).

Figure 4.9 Sample Performance Descriptors for Information Seeking Strategies

Create *criteria* based on the learning objectives to clearly indicate desired levels of success. Relevant criteria for Information Seeking Strategies include range and completeness, accuracy, and currency. For the sample lessons shared above, Colet Bartow created *performance descriptors* to distinguish among novice, nearing proficient, proficient, and advanced students on key criteria. Figure 4.9 is a more detailed table of assessment criteria that might be applied to skills related to Information Seeking Strategies.

The language in a performance description should be specific to the grade level and readily accessible to students and parents.

Reported

Two specific options for communicating performance information to students, other teachers, parents and caregivers, or administrators are the observation record and the report to parents.

The observation record is a short checklist that documents student accomplishments as well as what needs improving (see Figure 4.10).

Clearly, the "Notes" section is the most meaningful for students, teachers, and parents. Students learn from the recommendations and are able to revise and resubmit their work. Other teachers and parents are able to focus their help and attention on specific deficiencies.

Report to Parents

Communicating with parents and caregivers should be done on a regular basis. One simple action is to add the Big6 by the Month stage to your school's calendar to communicate with parents and teachers (see Figure 4.11).

Audience: Students Options: Observation Record	Evidence: Individuals select at least three sources. Criteria: At least three sources (two different types) are selected AND the students explain why (logically and accurately) they selected the sources (e.g., topical, current, trustworthy, precise, etc.).		
Name: Helen		**Date:**	**Assignment**
Novice	*Nearing Proficient*	*Proficient*	*Advanced*
E. Selects minimal relevant resources without explanation.	E. Selects some resources to solve the problem with incomplete explanation.	E. Selects and justifies appropriate resources to solve the problem.	E. Selects and justifies unique resources to solve the problem.
Notes: Three similar resources selected were appropriate to the assignment, but you did not give explanation for each of the three resources.—Please use complete sentences and give at least one specific reason for selecting. Let's review topical, current, trustworthy, preciseness as possible reasons for selection. Mrs. B.			

Big6 by the Month: Information Seeking Strategies (2011). Developed by Colet Bartow.

Figure 4.10 Sample Observation Record

Figure 4.11 Sample Calendar for November

	4th-grade students will be able to:	Questions to ask:
Sample Message for November: Dear Parents/Guardians: During the month of November, your student will work on a variety of projects and assignments. As part of each project, we will focus on Stage 2 of the Big6 information problem-solving model: Information Seeking Strategies. You can help reinforce these skills by asking them questions that relate to: 2.1 Determining all possible sources. 2.2 Selecting the best sources. The chart in this message details the skills students will practice and some questions you can ask to help students be successful as they complete assignments and projects. Please contact me if you have any questions. [insert contact information]	Construct a list of possible resources.	Have you thought about different types of resources? Examples of resources might include: reference materials, newspapers, websites, nonfiction books, personal interviews, audio files, video files, community resources, magazine search engines.
	Determine relevant resources to solve the problem or task.	How do you know that the resources you have chosen are the best?

Big6 by the Month: Information Seeking Strategies (2012). Developed by Colet Bartow.

Figure 4.12 Sample Report to Parents, Information Seeking Strategies

More extensive reporting of assessment and performance information can guide parents and caregivers to provide more specific and meaningful help to their children. For example, imagine parents being informed that their child did well in identifying sources but seems less sure of herself in explaining why one source is better than another. In addition, in a report to parents, the teachers provide a list of questions for parents to ask their children to hone their evaluation of sources skills (e.g., What makes a source trustworthy? How do you find out the source of factual information? Why do we value current, up-to-date information?).

Questions such as these can lead to more productive conversations about what students are expected to know and be able to do. The important thing is to encourage conversations between parents and students by providing substantive suggestions about how to talk about Information Seeking Strategies. These conversations can then serve to reinforce the skills learned in school and allow students to share their learning with confidence. See Figure 4.12 for a sample short report that provides specific, valuable information.

How you report is as important as what you are reporting. Consider whether or not your current reporting methods clearly communicate criteria for success, evidence of learning, and current status (of the student or of the program). Also, reporting need not be difficult or time-consuming. We recommend developing a straightforward template or format that will allow you to easily update and make changes month to month.

Summary

The Big6 by the Month program focuses on a "classic" information skill in the month of November: Information Seeking Strategies.

We begin with identifying ICT literacy and Common Core standards related to Information Seeking Strategies. These include standards pertinent to identifying a *variety* of information sources and *evaluating* them for their appropriateness and credibility. From the range of possible standards, we carefully *define* the most meaningful power objectives for each grade level.

Next, to make the program *predictable*, we create lesson plans in conjunction with local content assignments to address each of the grade level objectives. Assignments themselves can be more predictable if teachers use and students become familiar with a consistent format (one that is hopefully also consistent with the format and structure used on standardized tests).

Measurement follows, with determining the *evidence* and *criteria* by which students will be assessed. And finally, student success is *reported* to the students as well as their teachers, parents, and administrators.

Online Resources

Useful Sites: Evaluate Information Sources

"Know Your Major Information Sources," graphic, http://big6.com/media/freestuff/know-your-info-sources.gif

"Know Your Information Sources" Quiz (grades 7–12), by Susan McMullen, http://big6.com/media/freestuff/McMullenHandout1.pdf

"Evaluate Your Sources: Print and Website" (grades 7–12), by Marley Winningham, http://big6.com/media/freestuff/Marley_Big6_article2.pdf

"Information Seeking Strategies and Library Instruction," by Ru Story-Huffman, http://big6.com/pages/lessons/articles/big6-and-higher-ed-information-seeking-strategies-and-library-instruction.php

"Flipping the Library Classroom for Information Literacy," by Shannon Betts, http://connectlearningtoday.com/students-research-in-science-fair-collaboration/

"Critical Evaluation Information," by Kathy Schrock, http://www.schrockguide.net/critical-evaluation.html

"Thinking About World Wide Web Pages," by Janet Murray, http://janetsinfo.com/webeval1.html

TRAILS: Tools for Real-Time Assessment of Information Literacy Skills, http://www.trails-9.org

Chapter 5

"HIDE AND SEEK"

December:
Location & Access

3.1 Locate sources (intellectually and physically).

3.2 Find information within sources.

In This Chapter

- ❑ Introduction: Location & Access
- ❑ Defined: Standards and Grade Level Objectives
- ❑ Predictable: Lesson Ideas
- ❑ Measured: Performance Descriptors
- ❑ Reported: Report to Parents and Administrators
- ❑ Summary
- ❑ Online Resources

Introduction: Location & Access

Until very recently, searching for information wasn't easy. Search—particularly online search—was the highly skilled work of librarians and information professionals. Effective searches required expert knowledge of specialized sources. Of course, the World Wide Web changed all that. Today, even preschoolers know that if they want to find information about something, they can just "Google" it.

However, as educators and librarians, we know that there's a lot more to search than Google. Yes, the amount of information available on the web and the effectiveness and efficiency of Google are truly remarkable. Google is pervasive, and that's why learning about online searching today must begin with Google and how to search through the World Wide Web.

Many school districts subscribe to a database of periodicals, online encyclopedias, and special subjects, such as EBSCO, ProQuest, or Gale PowerSearch. In addition to being aware of the scope of possible sources, students need to learn how to locate and access these sources—digital and print—and the various commands, logic, and tools of searching as part of Big6 stage 3, Location & Access. Learning to assess the reliability and credibility of web-based resources and distinguish them from subscription periodicals is an important part of Information Seeking Strategies. Understanding Boolean logic and applying it to search actions is also an essential skill for all students to master by the time they enter high school.

Location & Access

    3.1 Locate sources (intellectually and physically)

    3.2 Find information within sources

Broadly, Location & Access includes two major actions: first, to find the information sources themselves (3.1), and then to get to the specific information within sources (3.2). Traditionally, we begin by instructing students how to locate information in the school library by using the card catalog or, more recently, its electronic counterpart.

For Location & Access 3.1, students need to be able to find the actual sources electronically or physically. For example, students should be able to determine where the sources are located: in the classroom, library, through the school's network, on the Internet, or some other places. We like to ask two basic questions:

- Where will students find the sources they need?
- Who can help students obtain the sources?

For online or digital tools, is the information itself available on the free web, from subscription databases, or in some other electronic or digital format? Students should also be aware of how the sources are organized in these places: alphabetically by topic or author, by the Dewey Decimal or Library of Congress classification system, or not at all.

And if the source is a person, can the student contact this person by telephone or e-mail, or is it best (or necessary) to meet and interview him or her face to face? Examples of 3.1 subskills relate to students being able to do the following:

- Locate sources in the library.
- Use a search engine on the Internet.
- Find sources by Dewey Decimal number.
- Use Boolean "and" to narrow a search.
- Use Boolean "or" to broaden a search.
- Find books about animals on their classroom bookshelves.
- Arrange to interview a community member.
- Select appropriate keywords.

Location & Access 3.2 refers to actually getting to the information in a given source. Once the source is located, students must find the specific information they need. This isn't the most glamorous of skills, but it is essential nevertheless. And there is a key to this stage—it's learning to search for and then use—the INDEX! This is the librarian's secret weapon: the index. Librarians and teachers have traditionally taught students about indexes, but doing so within the context of the Big6 process makes a lot more sense to children.

Examples of Location & Access 3.2 subskills relate to students being able to do the following:

- Use the search box within a particular website.
- Skim (or use "Find" with keywords) to find the specific relevant section on a website.
- Find the specific article or section of an article within an online source or system.
- Use the index in textbooks.
- Use a table of contents.
- Look up locations on a map or geographic information system (GIS).
- Use the search tools in *Wikipedia* and other online encyclopedias to get to the needed section.

There's also an interrelationship between Location & Access and Information Seeking Strategies. As explained above, basic searching is easy today; almost anyone can find a few okay/reasonable/good hits, and for many tasks this is sufficient. However, even expert searchers may come up empty-handed when using a particular source, so they reconsider their Information Seeking Strategies options, select a different source or system, and again engage in Location & Access. We want students to be very familiar and comfortable with the interplay between Information Seeking Strategies and Location & Access and also to gain sophistication over time.

The importance of Location & Access (and Information Seeking Strategies) skills are validated by the inclusion of questions that test these skills on the SAT and other standardized district, state, and national tests. Look for sample questions that ask students to choose among possible sources of information (Information Seeking Strategies) or ones that ask students to narrow or expand a search with *Boolean* operators.

The following sections further explain how to plan and implement practical and doable Location & Access instruction and learning in December to meet the needs of all students in your school.

Defined

In the December 2012 webinar, Mike noted that "the number one source of information that people (including students) turn to most is: OTHER PEOPLE. This was true 'pre-Web' and still holds true today as verified by Project Information Literacy in our 2010 study" (A. Head and M. Eisenberg, "Truth Be Told: How College Students Evaluate and Use Information in the Digital Age," Project Information Literacy Progress Report, November 1, 2010, University of Washington's Information School). When they do search the web, today's students tend to rely almost exclusively on Google to locate and access information.

You will want to encourage consideration of a wider range of sources as well as more effective Internet *search tools* and *techniques*. The Big6 by the Month program *defines* each stage of the Big6 in terms of standards augmented by grade level objectives or learning expectations.

Standards for Location & Access

Each of these sets of information and communication technology (ICT) literacy standards refers to effective Location & Access of information.

ICT Literacy Standards Related to Location & Access	
AASL	1.1.8 Demonstrate mastery of technology tools for *accessing* information and pursuing inquiry. 1.3.2 Seek divergent perspectives during information *gathering* and assessment.
ACRL	2.1 Selects the most appropriate investigative methods or information retrieval systems for *accessing* the needed information. 2.2 Constructs and implements effectively designed *search strategies*.
TRAILS	3. Develop, use, and revise *search strategies*.
ISTE NETS	3b. *Locate*, organize, analyze, evaluate, synthesize, and ethically use information from a variety of sources and media.

Compiled by Janet Murray from *AASL Standards for the 21st-Century Learner*, © 2007, American Association of School Librarians, http://www.ala.org/aasl/standards; "Information Literacy Competency Standards for Higher Education," © 2000, Association of College and Research Libraries, http://www.ala.org/ala/mgrps/divs/acrl/standards/informationliteracycompetency.cfm; TRAILS: Tools for Real-Time Assessment of Information Literacy Skills, http://www.trails-9.org/; and ISTE, *National Educational Technology Standards (NETS-S) for Students*. See "Big6™ Skills Aligned with ICT Literacy Standards," http://janetsinfo.com/Big6_ICT LitStds.htm.

Figure 5.1 ICT Literacy Standards Related to Location & Access

Teachers and students need to know that information literacy skills are important in all areas of the curriculum, not just as part of research. The Common Core State Standards Initiative provides a national set of guidelines describing what high school graduates must know and be able to do in order to succeed in entry-level college courses or the workplace. Some of these standards pertain directly to Location & Access (see Figure 5.2).

Common Core Standards Related to Location & Access	
Writing	2. Write informative/explanatory texts . . . through the effective *selection* . . . of content. 8. *Gather* relevant information from multiple print and digital sources. . . .
Mathematical Practices	5. Use appropriate tools strategically: . . . identify relevant external resources.

Compiled by Janet Murray and Colet Bartow from The Common Core State Standards Initiative, http://www.corestandards.org /the-standards. See also "Big6™ Skills Aligned with Common Core Standards," http://janetsinfo.com/Big6_CCSSIStds.htm.

Figure 5.2 Common Core Standards Related to Location & Access

Examine your state's content standards to find similar wording. (Use the *Standards Template* in the appendix or the electronic version online at https://sites.google.com/site/big6xthemonth/file-cabinet.)

As we did for Task Definition and Information Seeking Strategies, for Location & Access we again review the standards from the above sources as well as state and local standards and then identify the priority "power" Location & Access objectives for each grade level.

Grade Level Objectives

For each Big6 or Super3 stage, our goal as teachers, technology teachers, or teacher-librarians is to identify "power" information literacy goals and learning objectives for all students in our schools. These goals and objectives should link to relevant national or local learning standards. Figure 5.3 displays Montana's *Essential Learning Expectations for Information Literacy* related to Location & Access. Notice the progression of skills and distinctions between search *tools* and *techniques* as well as the particular tools associated with locating information within multiple resources.

Grade level objectives related to locating and accessing information might relate to each of these tools and techniques. Use the *Grade Level Objectives Template* in the "Templates" section of the appendices to create learning expectations for each grade level at your school.

Cross-Grade Objective	Grades					
	K	**1**	**2**	**3**	**4**	**5**
2.1 Locate sources.	A. Explore possible resources.#	A. Choose resources from a limited selection.	A. Locate major sections in the library.	A. Locate resources using search techniques.*	A. Construct a list of possible resources.	C. Identify and select useful resources.
2.1 Locate sources: *library catalog.*			B. Locate resources using a library catalog and/or database.	B. Locate resources using a library catalog and/or database.		

Cross-Grade Objective	Grades					
	K	1	2	3	4	5
2.1 Locate sources: *call number.*			C. Locate resources using a call number.	C. Locate resources using a call number.		
2.1 BM 8 Locate multiple resources using *search tools.*						A. Use search tools: vocabulary.^
2.1 BM 8 Locate multiple resources using search tools: *techniques.*						B. Use search techniques: vocabulary.*
2.3 Locate *information within the source* (vocabulary).	Author, illustrator, title page, copyright, table of contents.	Author, illustrator, title page, copyright, table of contents.	Author, illustrator, title page, copyright, table of contents.	Author, illustrator, title page, copyright, table of contents.	Author, illustrator, title page, copyright, table of contents.	
2.3 BM 8 Locate information within multiple resources.						Vocabulary.^

Cross-Grade Objective	Grades				
	6	7	8	9–10	11–12
2.1 BM 8 Locate multiple resources using *search tools.*	B. Use a variety of available search tools and methods.**	B. Use a variety of available search tools and methods.**	B. Use multiple search tools and methods.**	C. Demonstrate ability to access and search available print and nonprint material.	C. Demonstrate ability to access and search available print and nonprint material.
2.1 BM 8 Locate multiple resources using search tools; *techniques.*	C. Use search techniques### to locate resources.	C. Use search techniques### to locate resources.	C. Use a variety of search techniques### to locate resources.	D. Demonstrate ability to access and search available digital resources.	D. Demonstrate ability to access and search available digital resources.

Figure 5.3 Grade Level Objectives Related to Location & Access (*Continues on next page*)

Cross-Grade Objective	Grades				
	6	**7**	**8**	**9–10**	**11–12**
2.1 BM 8 Locate multiple resources.	D. Locate resources (e.g., call number, URL, link).	D. Locate resources (e.g., call number, URL, link).	D. Locate a variety of resources (e.g., call number, URL, link).	H. Perform an advanced search using search engine(s) and digital database(s).	E. Narrow search results independently using limiters within a digital search.
2.3 BM 8 Locate information within multiple resources.	A. Use *glossaries* and *tables of contents*.	A. Use glossaries and tables of contents.	A. Use glossaries and tables of contents.		
2.3 BM 8 Locate information within multiple resources.	B. Use print *indexes*. C. Recognize digital indexes.	B. Use print and digital indexes.	B. Use multiple print and digital indexes.	A. Sort within selected digital databases.	A. Sort within selected digital databases.
2.3 BM 8 Locate information within multiple resources.	D. Identify *keywords* and keyword phrases by skimming and scanning.	C. Identify keywords and keyword phrases by skimming and scanning.	C. Identify keywords and keyword phrases by skimming and scanning.	B. Choose keywords to locate and cross reference information.	B. Choose keywords to locate and cross reference information.

Compiled by Janet Murray from Montana's *Essential Learning Expectations for Information Literacy*, http://www.opi.mt.gov/pdf/Standards/10FebELE_LibMedia.xls.

BM = benchmark

print, nonprint, digital, community resources

* for example, keywords, Boolean/limiter, phrase, title, author, subject

^ subject directory, database, Boolean, skimming, scanning, digital indexes, glossaries, tables of contents

**library catalog, indexes, search engines, subject directory, Boolean searches, digital databases

keywords, Boolean/limiters, phrase, title, author and subject

Figure 5.3 Grade Level Objectives Related to Location & Access (*continued*)

Predictable

By December, the *predictable* Big6 by the Month program is well under way, with students already receiving formal instruction and improving their skills in Task Definition and Information Seeking Strategies. For December, we continue the program by focusing on Location & Access. As for previous months, we encourage you to develop a plan to fulfill the defined objectives for Location & Access consistent with your school's calendar, organization, and schedule. We again link to the classroom curriculum of every student by identifying one or two major assignments for each grade and teacher, then developing Location & Access lessons targeted to these assignments and related subject area units.

Lesson Ideas for Location & Access

Location & Access

3.1 Locate sources

3.2 Find information within sources

To locate information on the World Wide Web, students will use search engines, search strategies (tools and techniques), and subject directories. Subject directories are useful because they annotate websites that have been evaluated and organize them hierarchically by topic. KidsClick (http://kidsclick.org) "is a web search site designed for kids by librarians—with kid-friendly results." KidsClick is especially useful for younger students because it indicates the reading level of the sites retrieved. The Internet Public Library's (http://www.ipl.org/) "For Kids" page includes a section of resources for parents and teachers. Both of these sites also have "search" boxes to encourage students to develop appropriate keywords. The Multnomah County Library Homework Center (http://www.mult colib.org/homework/) includes links to "trusted online resources" (alternatives to *Wikipedia*) as well as a subject directory of websites.

One way to introduce students to subject directories is to have them compare the results of the same search in several different directories. Point out that searching for "bears" by starting with the category "animals" eliminates extraneous sites like those pertaining to the Chicago Bears football team. Direct students to point and click on successive categories rather than type in the search box and to record their exploratory path.

Other valuable search tools and techniques to incorporate in your information literacy grade level objectives include databases and digital indexes, Boolean limiters, and advanced search strategies. Direct students to compare the results of the same search in several different search engines, then ask them to analyze which search engine gave them the best results.

The first sample lesson is for the Super3—focusing on the difference between "*browse*" and "*search*" under the Middle-DO stage of the Super3 (see Figure 5.4).

Super3™ Stage:	DO
Grade Level:	K–I
GL Objective:	Understand the difference between browse and search and be able to do each
Subject Area:	Science
Unit Focus:	Inventors and Inventions

Figure 5.4 Early Elementary DO Lesson in Context

Subject Area Lesson Goal: Students will choose from a listing on a website and view three (3) videos about key inventions of the 20th and 21st centuries (e.g., the World Wide Web, Play-Doh, cell phones, Apple PC, Lego).

Learning Activity: The instructor will explain the difference between "browsing" and "searching," using examples from retail stores, books, and the World Wide Web. Students will go to a special page on the school's website that includes videos about inventions from the last one hundred years. They have two tasks: (1) to browse through the videos (presented in random order) to select a video that is interesting and (2) to decide on an invention or inventor (from a printed list) and then to use the search box (provided) to locate the video. The teacher will debrief the class to identify the pros and cons of browsing and searching.

Assessment:

- Evidence: Worksheet that guides student work and includes places for students to indicate why they like or don't like browsing or searching.
- Criteria: Completed worksheet. Valid reasons for liking or disliking browse or search.

Another way to introduce young children to the distinction between "browse" and "search" is to connect this aspect of the Super3 DO to choosing a book to check out of the library. Some children will "browse" the shelves and select a book based on the attractiveness of its cover. Other children have already identified a favorite author or series and will "search" for another book in the series by going to the card catalog or the appropriate alphabetical section.

Examples of Big6 Location & Access lessons in the context of classroom assignments follow. Note that these are presented in Big6 order (3.1 then 3.2) rather than by grade level. See Figures 5.5 and 5.6.

Big6™ Stage:	Location & Access: 3.1 Locate all sources
Grade Level:	7–8
GL Objective:	Locate multiple resources using search tools
Subject Area:	Science
Unit Focus:	Body Health

Figure 5.5 Secondary Location & Access (3.1) Lesson in Context

Subject Area Lesson Goal: Students will individually compose an essay about two possible health risks to the body (e.g., illegal drugs, alcohol, high fat diet, tobacco) and will discuss at least two ways (two "how" and two "why") to avoid each risk.

Learning Activity: Students will use search techniques (Boolean/limiters, phrases, titles, keywords, subjects) to locate selected sources.

Assessment:

- Evidence: Essay.
- Criteria: Students consistently apply search techniques to locate selected sources.

Big6™ Stage:	Location & Access: 3.2 Find information within sources
Grade Level:	1–2
GL Objective:	3.2 Locate information within the source (vocabulary)
Subject Area:	Language Arts—Reading
Unit Focus:	Book Knowledge: Text Features

Figure 5.6 Elementary Location & Access (3.2) Lesson in Context

Subject Area Lesson Goal: Students will select five (5) new vocabulary words from a nonfiction book and will use the index or glossary to locate the meaning of each word.

Learning Activity: Students will use text features (table of contents, index, glossary) to locate and define vocabulary words from the nonfiction book they are currently reading.

Assessment:

- Evidence: On worksheet, student circles the text feature(s) used. Verbal explanation by student.
- Criteria: Student completes the worksheet. Student is able to explain what at least one text feature does.

Use the *Lesson Plan Template* in the "Templates" section of the appendices or online at https://sites.google.com/site/big6xthemonth/file-cabinet to develop lessons.

Measured

Students and teachers, as well as parents and administrators, need to know whether or not students have achieved the desired Location & Access goals and objectives. *Evidence* of performance on Location & Access skills can be found in a worksheet, checklist, or self-assessment or as part of the overall assignment.

With evidence selected, we can identify *criteria* based on the learning objectives, such as degrees of completeness, accuracy, or logical reasoning. The number, type, range, and quality of sources are also possible criteria during Big6 stage Location & Access. The language in a performance description should be specific to the grade level and readily accessible to students and parents. Figure 5.7 is a summary table of assessment criteria that might be applied to the Location & Access lessons above.

Grade Level	Specific GLO	Big6™ Stage	Subject Area	Assignment	Evidence	Criteria
K/1	Browse vs. Search	Super3 = DO	Science	Videos of inventors and inventions	Worksheet	Complete, accurate, logical
7/8	Advanced Search	3.1	Science	Essay: two health risks and ways to avoid	Sources cited in the essay	Sources are relevant and appropriate
1/2	Use text features to locate words in text	3.2	Language arts and reading	Identify and define five words.	Worksheet or verbal explanation	Completeness; able to explain one text feature

Figure 5.7 Assessment Criteria for Location & Access Lessons

Colet Bartow created sample *performance descriptors* to distinguish among novice, nearing proficient, proficient, and advanced students learning Location & Access skills. For kindergarten students, the descriptors in Figure 5.8 apply to locating sources and finding information within them (Super3 stage DO; Big6 stages 3.1 and 3.2).

Seventh- and eighth-grade students are more sophisticated in their Location & Access strategies, but variations in quality of performance can still be identified, as in Figure 5.9.

Performance descriptors can be adapted to provide self-assessment tools as students gather information. The criteria appear at the top of the worksheet in Figure 5.10.

The self-assessment worksheet (see Figure 5.10) and/or the search worksheets provide evidence of student achievement.

Novice	Nearing Proficient	Proficient	Advanced
DO Locate a resource by browsing with limited success.	Select a resource by browsing.	Select resources by both browsing and searching.	Select resources by precise and accurate searching.
3.1 A. Explore fiction and nonfiction resources with limited success.	A. Explore fiction and nonfiction resources with some errors.	A. Explore fiction and nonfiction resources.	A. Explore fiction and nonfiction resources with precision and accuracy.
3.2 A. Identify few parts of a book.	A. Identify some parts of a book.	A. Identify basic parts of a book.	A. Identify parts of a book beyond basics.
B. View or listen for information rarely.	B. View or listen for information some of the time.	B. View and listen for information.	B. View or listen for information with attention to detail.

Big6 by the Month: Location & Access (2011).

Figure 5.8 Sample Performance Descriptors for DO/Location & Access (Kindergarten)

Novice	Nearing Proficient	Proficient	Advanced
3.1 A. Use single search tool.	A. Use multiple search tools.	A. Use multiple search tools and methods.	A. Independently use multiple search tools and methods.
B. Use one preferred search technique.	B. Identify a variety of search techniques.	B. Use a variety of search techniques to locate resources.	B. Apply search techniques to follow appropriate leads to additional sources.
C. Return to previously used resource.	C. Locate limited number of resources.	C. Locate a variety of resources.	C. Use advanced search tools to locate inter-related resources.
3.2 A. Use index, glossaries, and tables of contents infrequently.	A. Use index, glossaries, and tables of contents sometimes.	A. Use index, glossaries, and tables of contents.	A. Use index, glossaries, and tables of contents consistently.
B. Rely on single reading strategy to locate information.	B. Demonstrate general understanding of locating keywords and keyword phrases.	B. Identify keywords and keyword phrases by skimming and scanning.	B. Applies skimming and scanning to an entire resource to locate information.

Big6 by the Month: Location & Access (2012).

Figure 5.9 Sample Performance Descriptors for Location & Access (Grades 7–8)

- Novice: 1–3 items for each source
- Nearing Proficient: 4–6 items for each source
- Proficient: 7–10 items for each source
- Advanced: 11+ items for each source

3.1 Locate sources	Source 1	Source 2	Source 3
Card Catalog Search 　Author 　Title 　Call Number 　Subject			
Subject Directories			
Search Engines			
URLs			
Databases			
3.2 Find information within sources	Source 1	Source 2	Source 3
Index Entries			
Table of Contents Entries			
Glossary Entries			
Keywords/Keyword Phrases			

Big6 by the Month: Location & Access (2012). Developed by Colet Bartow.

Figure 5.10 Sample Self-Assessment Tool for Location & Access

Reported

As emphasized, a monthly (or quarterly) report to parents will keep them informed about the ICT literacy program and classroom, technology, and library activities that demonstrate the value of your ICT instructional efforts.

At the very least, consider adding Big6 by the Month Location & Access to your school's calendar so that the ICT program is consistently and regularly communicated to parents, teachers, and administrators (see Figure 5.11).

Parents and caregivers will also benefit from receiving specific information on how they can help their children succeed. Sometimes, a list of questions can help lead to more productive conversations about what students are expected to know and be able to do. The important thing is to encourage conversation between parents and students.

For example, in December we would let parents know that we are working with students on the difference between search and browse, about how Google relates to other search tools, using keywords, indexes, and tables of contents. We can encourage parents to start conversations that serve to reinforce the skills of Location & Access and give students the opportunity to share their learning with confidence. See Figure 5.12.

In assessing your reporting actions, consider whether or not your current reporting methods clearly communicate

- criteria for success,
- evidence of learning, and
- current status.

December is Location & Access Month

	Sunday	Monday	Tuesday	Wednesday	Thursday	Friday	Saturday
		Winter Holiday					
	3.1 Locate sources. 3.2 Find information within sources.						

Figure 5.11 Sample Calendar for December

Sample Message for December:	*4th-grade Students will be able to:*	*Questions to ask:*
Dear Parents/Guardians: During the month of December, your child and the other students will work on a variety of projects and assignments. As part of each project, we will focus on stage 3 of the Big6 information problem-solving model, Location & Access. You can help reinforce these skills by asking your student questions that relate to: 3.1 Locating sources. 3.2 Finding information within sources. The chart in this message explains the skills your student will practice and some questions you can ask to help your child be successful as he or she completes assignments and projects. Please contact me if you have any questions. [insert contact information]	Locate multiple sources of information in a variety of formats.	What types of resources are you using for your project? Have you thought about using an encyclopedia/website/non-fiction book/primary source? Why is Google a search tool and not a browser?
	Find information within a variety of sources, using a variety of strategies.	What strategies or tools are you using to find information in a specific type of resource? What keywords are you using to zero in on the information you need? Have you found information by using a table of contents/ glossary or index? How can you use Google to find information within a website?

Big6 by the Month: Location & Access (2012). Developed by Colet Bartow.

Figure 5.12 Sample Report to Parents, Location & Access

Do your reports help students, parents, other teachers, and administrators grasp the full scope, depth, and importance of the ICT literacy program? How might you improve your reporting?

Summary

The Big6 by the Month program emphasizes Location & Access skills in the month of December. We recommend targeting ICT literacy and Common Core standards by creating grade level objectives related to locating sources using a variety of *search tools* and *techniques* and *finding* information within the sources using indexes, tables of contents, glossaries, keywords, and skimming and scanning.

Create lesson plans based on classroom content assignments that emphasize each of the Super3 or Big6 grade level objectives. Make assignments and activities *predictable* by using a consistent format—one that highlights the ICT learning objectives and the content objectives. Clearly identify the *evidence* and *criteria* by which students will be assessed and *report* ICT program activities to parents, administrators, and other educators.

Online Resources

Useful Sites: Location & Access

"Location and Access: Evaluate Sources Early and Often," by Marley Winningham, http://big6.com/pages /lessons/articles/location-and-access-evaluate-sources-early-and-often.php

Big6 Location & Access (YouTube video grades 7–9), https://www.youtube.com/watch?v=-0NjVdBkXvE

"Location and Access: Threading the Needle" (secondary), by Ru Story-Huffman, http://big6.com/pages/lessons /lessons/location-and-access-threading-the-needle.php

Have students compare their results using different search engines (by Janet Murray), http://janetsinfo.com /srchwk1.html

"Choose the Best Search for Your Information Need," by Debbie Abilock, http://www.noodletools.com/debbie /literacies/information/5locate/adviceengine.html

"Finding Information on the Internet" (useful for adults)—UC Berkeley Tutorial, http://www.lib.berkeley.edu /TeachingLib/Guides/Internet/FindInfo.html

Useful Sites: Subject Directories

Use a subject directory of evaluated resources that organizes information hierarchically:

- The Internet Public Library has merged with Librarians' Internet Index, http://www.ipl.org/
- KidsClick, http://kidsclick.org
- Multnomah County Library Homework Center, http://www.multcolib.org/homework/

Have students compare their results using different subject directories (by Janet Murray) at http://janetsinfo.com /subjwkmid.html.

Chapter 6

"EUREKA! I'VE GOT IT"
(ARCHIMEDES)
January:
Use of Information

4.1 Engage (e.g., read, hear, view, touch) information.

4.2 Extract relevant information.

In This Chapter

❑ Introduction: Use of Information

❑ Defined: Standards and Grade Level Objectives

❑ Predictable: Lesson Ideas, Application to Statewide Exams, Citing Sources

❑ Measured: Performance Descriptors

❑ Reported: Standards-Based Rubrics, Report to Parents

❑ Summary

❑ Online Resources

Introduction: Use of Information

The previous two Big6 stages (Information Seeking Strategies and Location & Access) were focused on identifying where to find and gather information from sources. Now, in Use of Information, it's time to recognize what information is relevant to the task and to extract the information in some useful way, such as by taking notes. Students should allow plenty of time to read and understand the information they find as well as set aside any information that does not help with their tasks.

Use of Information

4.1 Engage (e.g., read, hear, view, touch)

4.2 Extract relevant information

Ultimately, to gain useful and meaningful information from a source, students need to read, listen to, or view (touch, taste, sense) information in some form. This is Big6 stage 4.1, "engaging" the information, and it is crucially important. The widespread emphasis on reading comprehension and student performance on standardized tests attests to the importance of this stage.

Examples of **Use of Information 4.1** include students being able to do the following:

- Listen attentively to directions.
- Watch a weather report for local storm conditions.
- Interview a community helper for a project.
- Read a topographic map.
- Interact with a website.

In Big6 stage 4.2, students determine the "relevance" of information when they read, listen to, or watch effectively. Even when students do locate sources and find appropriate information, they must be able to read and understand, listen effectively, or watch for key concepts and examples relevant to their tasks. "Extracting information" involves taking the information with you in some way. Students might take notes (electronic or written), copy and paste information, fill out a worksheet, download a file or photo, take a photo, record, or sometimes just remember the information.

Examples of **Use of Information 4.2** include students being able to do the following:

- Copy and paste main points into a word processing or PowerPoint document:
  - Main idea sentences
  - Main idea phrases, headings
  - Thesis statements
  - Supporting ideas
  - Action words
  - Nouns
- Recognize "juicy" information:
  - Relevant text
  - Diagrams
  - Charts with major ideas
  - Explanations
  - Examples
- Look for information patterns:
  - Relevance/important information
  - Graphics
  - Charts, tables, graphs
  - Listed by date, alphabetically, or in some other order
- Notice expert vocabulary:
  - Keywords
  - Jargon
  - Terms

Students, particularly younger ones, can become bogged down when using an information source because everything seems valuable and important. Here are some "tips" to share with students to help them be effective as well as save time and effort. These tips are helpful for students in any context, including the reading comprehension parts of standardized tests.

Tip 1: Be Choosy. Encourage students not to copy and paste or highlight every sentence. It will be too hard for students to tell which ideas are main ideas and which ones are minor points.

Tip 2: Students: Ask yourself! Remind students to continually ask themselves: "What is the task? What details do I need in order to complete the task?"

Tip 3: Read the questions first! If your students must read a long text passage in order to answer test questions, or questions at the end of a chapter, have them read the questions first. Students who know the questions before they begin to read will notice the answers more quickly in their reading.

Tip 4: Code it! Suggest that students develop and use a personal coding system. Whether using digital or print copies, students can put stars, *X*s, exclamation points, letters, numbers, or other marks within the text to make information easier to review later. A personal code can help students quickly sort main points, minor ideas, examples, and vocabulary words. Some students prefer a color code system, using colored highlighters for print sources or online highlighting for digital.

Tip 5: Cite when you copy and paste. Copying and pasting information from an electronic source is fine. However, students will need to cite the source of the information. It's much easier and less time-consuming if students record the citation of the source while they are taking notes rather than trying to do so later.

These tips relate directly to the standards, lessons, and assessments explained in more detail below.

Defined

Plan a school-wide focus on **Use of Information** for the month of January. Once students locate the relevant and credible information sources they need to complete an assignment, they will extract the most useful information. The Big6 by the Month program *defines* each stage of the Big6 in terms of standards augmented by grade level objectives or learning expectations.

Standards for Use of Information

Each of these sets of information and communication technology (ICT) literacy standards emphasizes the importance of ethical use of information. Notice the references to *analyzing* and *organizing* information as well as *legal* and *responsible use* in Figure 6.1.

ICT Literacy Standards Related to Use of Information	
AASL	2.1.1 Apply critical-thinking skills (**analysis**, synthesis, evaluation, **organization**) to information and knowledge. 1.3.3 Follow *ethical* and *legal* guidelines in gathering and *using information*.
ACRL	2.5 **Extracts**, **records**, and **manages** the information and its sources. 5.2 Follows *laws*, regulations, institutional policies, and etiquette related to the access and *use of information* resources.
TRAILS	5. Recognize how to *use information responsibly, ethically*, and *legally*.
NETS-S	4c. **Collect** and **analyze** data to identify solutions and/or make informed decisions. 5a. Advocate and practice safe, *legal*, and *responsible use of information* and technology.

Compiled by Janet Murray from *AASL Standards for the 21st-Century Learner*, © 2007, American Association of School Librarians, http://www.ala.org/aasl/standards; "Information Literacy Competency Standards for Higher Education," © 2000, Association of College and Research Libraries, http://www.ala.org/ala/mgrps/divs/acrl/standards/informationliteracycompetency.cfm; TRAILS: Tools for Real-Time Assessment of Information Literacy Skills, http://www.trails-9.org/; and ISTE, National Educational Technology Standards (NETS-S) for Students.

Figure 6.1 ICT Literacy Standards Related to Use of Information

When we teach students how to use the information they have located for an assignment, it is critically important to focus on both aspects of these standards, briefly defined as *taking notes* and *citing sources*.

Teachers and students need to know that information literacy skills are important in all areas of the curriculum, not just as part of research. The Common Core State Standards Initiative provides a national set of guidelines to describe what high school graduates must know and be able to do in order to succeed in entry-level college courses or the workplace. Some of these guidelines pertain directly to both substages of Big6 stage 4, Use of Information (see Figure 6.2).

Related Common Core Standards	4.1 Engage information
Reading	1. **Read closely** to determine what the text says explicitly 4. **Interpret** words and phrases as they are used in a text
Reading: Informational Text	4. Determine the **meaning** of words and phrases as they are used in a text, including figurative, connotative, and technical meanings.
Reading: Science and Technical Subjects	2. Determine the **central ideas** or conclusions of a text.
Writing	8. **Gather** relevant information from multiple print and digital sources
Speaking and Listening	3. **Evaluate** a speaker's point of view, reasoning, and use of evidence and rhetoric.
Mathematical Practices	2. **Reason** abstractly and quantitatively: . . . create a coherent representation of the problem at hand.

Related Common Core Standards	4.2 Extract information
Reading	5. **Analyze** the structure of texts. 9. **Analyze** how two or more texts address similar themes or topics.
Reading: Informational Text	2. Determine a central idea of a text and how it is conveyed through particular details; provide a **summary** of the text distinct from personal opinions or judgments.
Reading: History and Social Studies	2. Determine the central ideas or information of a primary or secondary source; provide an accurate **summary** of the source distinct from prior knowledge or opinions.
Writing	2. Write informative/explanatory texts to examine and convey complex ideas and information clearly and accurately through the effective **selection**, **organization**, and **analysis** of content. 8. Integrate the information while *avoiding plagiarism*.
Mathematical Practices	5. Use appropriate tools strategically: . . . make sound decisions about when tools might be helpful . . . use technological tools.

Compiled by Janet Murray and Colet Bartow from The Common Core State Standards Initiative, http://www.corestandards.org/the-standards. See also "Big6™ Skills Aligned with Common Core Standards," http://janetsinfo.com/Big6_CCSSIStds.htm.

Figure 6.2 Common Core Standards Related to Use of Information

You will notice many more Common Core standards related to Big6 stage 4, Use of Information, and Big6 stage 5, Synthesis, than to the other Big6 stages. However, we believe that students will do a much better job of extracting information (taking notes) and organizing it (Synthesis) if they have first learned to clearly define their assignment (Big6 stage 1, Task Definition), evaluate sources of information (Big6 stage 2, Information Seeking Strategies), and locate sources efficiently and effectively (Big6 stage 3, Location & Access). Then their note taking is more purposeful and their notes relate more directly to their topic. If students self-evaluate their project and their process (Big6 stage 6, Evaluation), their subsequent attempts to gather reliable and credible information will be more successful.

Examine your state's content standards to find similar wording. (Use the *Standards Template* in the "Templates" section of the appendices or the electronic version online at https://sites.google.com/site/big6xthemonth /file-cabinet.)

Grade Level Objectives

For each Big6 or Super3 stage, our goal as teachers, technology teachers, or teacher-librarians is to identify "power" information literacy goals and learning objectives for all students in our school. These goals and objectives should link to relevant national or local learning standards. Figure 6.3 displays Montana's *Essential Learning Expectations for Information Literacy* related to Use of Information. Notice the progression of skills and the several strategies

Cross-Grade Objective	Grades					
	K	1	2	3	4	5
2.3 Locate information within the source: *keywords.*	B. View and listen for information.	B. View and listen for information.	B. Read, view, and listen for information.	B. Read, view, or listen for information.	B. Skim and/ or scan for information.	B. Locate and summarize relevant information.
2.4 Extract information from resources: *main ideas.*	B. Explore main ideas.	B. Discuss main ideas and details.	B. Identify main ideas and details.	B. Recognize main ideas and details.	B. Recognize main ideas and details.	B. Locate and summarize relevant information.
2.4 Extract information from resources: *purpose.*	D. Listen and view for purpose.	D. Read and listen for purpose.	D. Construct meaning from text by reading for purpose.	D. Construct meaning from text by reading for purpose.	D. Construct meaning from text by reading for purpose.	A. Read, listen, and view with guided purpose.
2.4 Extract information from resources: *take notes.*	E. Listen and identify relevant information.	E. Listen and identify relevant information.	E. Summarize information using appropriate tools (e.g., graphic organizer).	E. Identify relevant information (e.g., through note taking).	E. Compile information (e.g., through note taking, graphic organizers).	C. Use teacher-provided note-taking method to transfer information.

Figure 6.3 Grade Level Objectives Related to Use of Information (*Continues*)

Cross-Grade Objective	Grades					
	K	1	2	3	4	5
2.4 Extract information from resources: *cite sources.*	G. Credit sources.	G. Credit sources.	F. Credit sources.	G. Cite sources.	G. Cite sources.	D. Cite each source.

Cross-Grade Objective	6	7	8	9–10	11–12
2.4 BM 8 Extract information from multiple resources: *purpose.*	A. Read, listen, and view with guided purpose.	A. Read, listen, and view with purpose.	A. Read, listen, and view with purpose.	A. Read, listen, and view to make inferences.	A. Read, listen, and view to make inferences.
2.4 BM 8 Extract information from multiple resources: *relevance.*	B. Summarize and paraphrase relevant information.	B. Summarize and paraphrase relevant information.	A. Read, listen, and view with purpose.	B. Gather information relevant to the formulated questions.	B. Gather information relevant to the formulated questions.
2.4 BM 8 Extract information from multiple resources: *summarize and paraphrase.*	B. Summarize and paraphrase relevant information.	B. Summarize and paraphrase relevant information.	B. Recognize the differences among summarizing, paraphrasing, and/or direct quotation.	C. Determine the correct usage of summaries, paraphrases, and direct quotations.	C. Summarize, paraphrase, and/or quote facts and details.
2.4 BM 8 Extract information from multiple resources: *cite sources.*	C. Cite each source.	C. Cite each source.	C. Cite each source.	D. Cite each source.	D. Cite each source.
2.4 BM 8 Extract information from multiple resources: *take notes.*	D. Use note taking to transfer information.	D. Use note taking to transfer information.	D. Transfer information through note taking.	2.5 A. Sort and categorize gathered information (e.g., graphic organizers, note cards, outline).	2.5 A. Sort and categorize gathered information (e.g., graphic organizers, note cards, outline).

Compiled by Janet Murray from Montana's *Essential Learning Expectations for Information Literacy,* http://www.opi.mt.gov/pdf /Standards/10FebELE_LibMedia.xls.

BM = benchmark

Figure 6.3 Grade Level Objectives Related to Use of Information (*continued*)

for extracting information from multiple resources (identify keywords, main ideas, purpose, take notes) as well as the emphasis on citing sources.

Use the *Grade Level Objectives Template* in the "Templates" section of the appendices to create learning expectations for each grade level at your school.

Predictable

In previous chapters, we've explained how to make the Big6 by the Month program *predictable* by devoting each month's program to a particular stage of the Super3 or Big6 Skills. As for other months, we emphasize two contexts for the predictable program: Use of Information as part of the overall Big6 process and Use of Information lessons tied to existing classroom and subject area assignments. Here, we offer lesson ideas for Use of Information.

Lesson Ideas for Use of Information

Building on the grade level objectives above, Use of Information has two substages and a range of specific skills within each:

4.1 Engage the information

- Read (view, listen, observe) for purpose
- Skim and scan
- Identify main ideas
- Determine relevance and credibility

4.2 Extract relevant and credible information

- Take notes
- Cite sources
- Distinguish among summarizing, paraphrasing, and using direct quotations

The first step in taking useful notes is Big6 4.1, Engage the information. As students select information resources, they need to read carefully with the purpose of the assignment firmly in mind. When we teach students to read, we direct them to identify main ideas, skim, and scan; these techniques are especially applicable when they prepare to extract information. "Reading for Information: The Trash 'n' Treasure Method of Teaching Notetaking," by Barbara Jansen (http://www.big6.com/media/Jansen.ReadingforInformationTTnotetakingjansen.pdf), offers a methodical approach that many teachers and teacher-librarians have used successfully. Students also need to practice listening attentively, taking notes from video resources or speakers.

Graphic organizers include a variety of designs that can help students take notes effectively. One of Janet's online students created the graphic organizer in Figure 6.4 to guide second graders to take notes about giraffes. Note that she required two sources, distinguished by both color and shape. Even young children can learn to separate information according to the source in which they found it.

Technology offers us some valuable and less tedious alternatives to taking notes on 3-by-5 cards. Mike Eisenberg suggests the PowerPoint template in Figure 6.5.

Students can sort the PowerPoint "note slides" in a logical order to compose an outline or write a report and then create a bibliography from the saved citations.

Following is an example of a lesson plan using PowerPoint "note slides" in the context of a classroom assignment (see Figure 6.6).

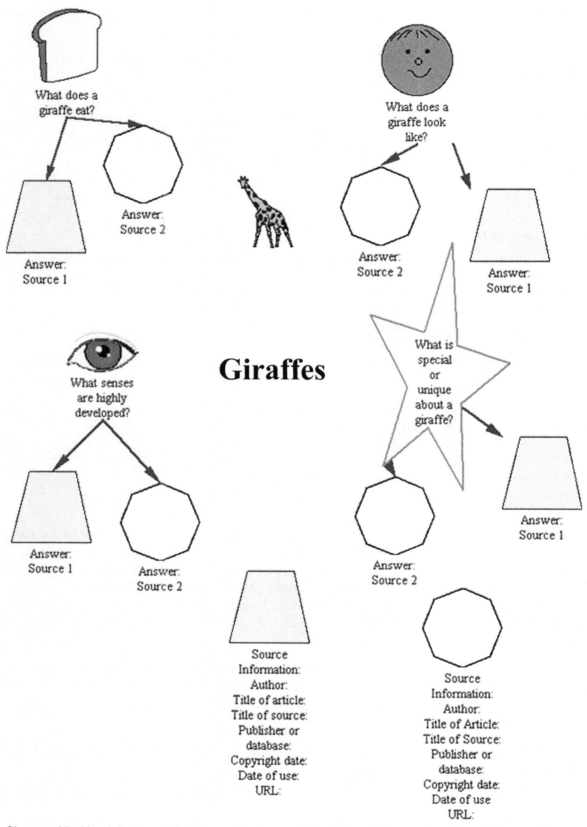

What does a giraffe eat?

Answer: Source 1

Answer: Source 2

What does a giraffe look like?

Answer: Source 2

Answer: Source 1

Giraffes

What senses are highly developed?

Answer: Source 1

Answer: Source 2

What is special or unique about a giraffe?

Answer: Source 2

Answer: Source 1

Source Information:
Author:
Title of article:
Title of source:
Publisher or database:
Copyright date:
Date of use:
URL:

Source Information:
Author:
Title of Article:
Title of Source:
Publisher or database:
Copyright date:
Date of use:
URL:

Christine Markley, Librarian, Washington Elementary School, Barto, PA; reprinted from Murray, *Achieving Educational Standards Using the Big6.*

Figure 6.4 Graphic Organizer for Note Taking

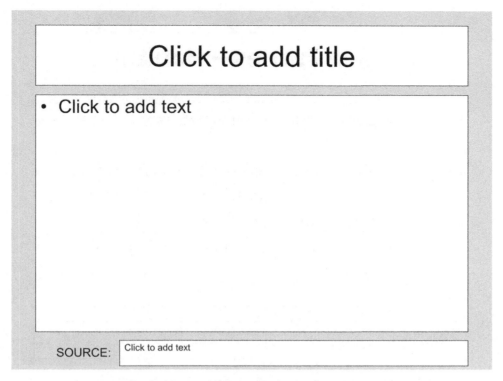

Figure 6.5 PowerPoint Template for Taking Notes

Big6™ Stage:	Use of Information: 4.2 Extract information
Grade Level:	4
GL Objective:	Take notes using digital tools
Subject Area:	Science
Unit Focus:	Types of animals

Figure 6.6 Elementary Use of Information (4.2) Lesson in Context

Subject Area Lesson Goal: To become familiar with animal vocabulary and to provide an example for each animal type. VOCABULARY: invertebrates, arachnids, crustaceans, insects, mollusks, sponges, vertebrates, reptiles, amphibians, mammals.

Learning Activity:

1. Students will work in teams of three to define specific vocabulary regarding animals.

2. Definitions will be recorded into "note slides" using PowerPoint. (See Figure 6.7.)

3. On each slide, teams will include a definition, example, and the source of their information.

Assessment:

- Evidence: Completed PowerPoint slides.

- Criteria: (1) Able to use PowerPoint—add slides, enter information. (2) Completeness—three parts to each slide. (3) Accuracy—correct definition, example. (4) Source—relevant and credible.

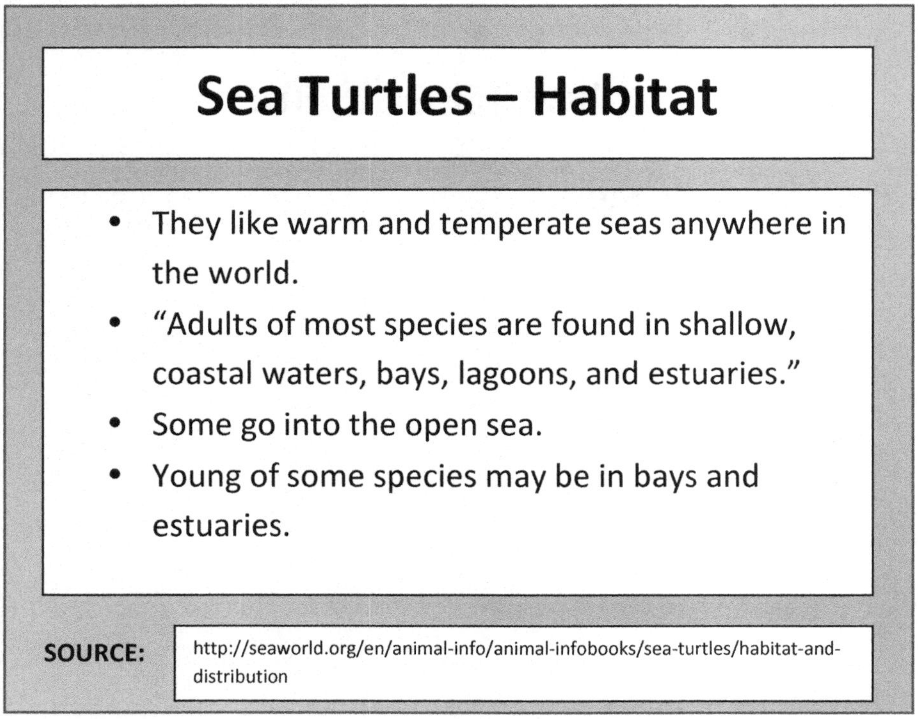

Figure 6.7 Sample PowerPoint "Note Slide"

There are other online resources available for electronic note taking, including the following:

- NoodleTools, http://noodletools.com/
- Evernote, http://evernote.com/
- OneNote, http://office.microsoft.com/en-us/onenote

Digital note taking and combining notes from many different online and print sources is a challenge for students at all levels today—even college. By providing lessons on digital note taking, the ICT literacy program can play a major role in helping students to develop effective and efficient note-taking habits.

When teaching students to extract information, it is also important to distinguish among *paraphrasing, summarizing*, and *quoting*. Following is a sample lesson plan focusing on use of information skills (see Figure 6.8).

Big6™ Stage:	*Use of Information: 4.1 Engage; 4.2 Extract*
Grade Level:	10–12
GL Objective:	Paraphrase for note taking
Subject Area:	Language arts
Unit Focus:	Writing

Figure 6.8 Secondary Use of Information (4.1 and 4.2) Lesson in Context

Subject Area Lesson Goal:

1. To learn the differences among quoting, paraphrasing, and summarizing.
2. To practice paraphrasing.

Learning Activity:

1. Using the Purdue University Online Writing Lab material (https://owl.english.purdue.edu/owl/resource/563/01/), discuss the differences among quoting, paraphrasing, and summarizing.

2. Practice paraphrasing and summarizing using the Purdue University Online Writing Lab materials (http://owl.english.purdue.edu/owl/resource/619/1/).

Assessment:

- Evidence: Discussion notes, sample paraphrased and summarized selections.
- Criteria: Accurately identify quote, paraphrase, and summarization. Accurately paraphrase from an example.

Use the *Lesson Plan Template* in the "Templates" section of the appendices to develop lessons.

Use of Information Skills Applied to Statewide Exams

As explained, reading comprehension is a major part of Use of Information. We can help students improve their reading comprehension skills by considering ways to teach use of information skills that are essential to successful performance on statewide exams (see Figure 6.9).

Grade Level	Specific GLE Skill/Tool/ Technique	Big6™ Stage	Subject Area	Assignment	Evidence	Criteria
3	Read, view, or listen for information.	4.1	English or language arts.	Practice statewide reading comprehension exams; give keywords to find.	Highlighted or underlined reading passage.	Accuracy: matched keywords and highlighted answers in passage.
4	Skim and/or scan for information.	4.1	English or language arts.	Practice statewide reading comprehension exams; give keywords to find.	Highlighted or underlined reading passage.	Accuracy: matched keywords and highlighted answers in passage.
6/7/8	Read, listen, and view with purpose.	4.1	English or language arts.	Practice statewide reading comprehension exams; give keywords to find.	Highlighted or underlined keywords in questions.	Accuracy: matched keywords and highlighted answers in passage.
3/4	Recognize main ideas and details.	4.2	English or language arts.	Practice statewide reading comprehension exams; identify keywords in questions and passages.	Highlighted or underlined keywords in questions and passages.	Accuracy: highlighted keywords and highlighted answers in passage.
6/7/8	Use note taking to transfer information.	4.2	English or language arts.	Practice statewide reading comprehension exams; identify keywords in questions and passages.	Highlighted or underlined keywords or notes for questions and passages.	Accuracy: highlighted keywords, notes, answers.

Figure 6.9 Use of Information Skills Applied to Statewide Exams

Citing Sources: Lesson Ideas

Mike Eisenberg believes that if you tell students to "give credit to your sources," it is more effective than threatening students with the academic or legal consequences of plagiarism. Janet Murray asks students how they would *feel* if someone else submitted their carefully produced art project. She thinks students can understand feeling "bad, sad, mad" if someone "stole" their work; then we can ask them to relate to the feelings of the author or composer or programmer whose hard work also deserves "credit."

We offer a range of lessons—from pre-K through high school—to help students learn the importance of crediting and how to do it effectively. The Super3 lesson in Figure 6.10 uses citing stickers (see Figure 6.11) that are available for purchase on the Big6 website, but you can just as easily create your own graphics to use or buy a rubber stamp of each of the four main types of resources: people, me-myself, computer, and books. The point is to get students to start crediting and citing early, creating an expectation or "culture of crediting" in your school. Later, we can get more sophisticated in our crediting/citing lessons—not focusing on the mechanics of using APA or MLA but continuing to emphasize why, when, and how to cite.

Super3™ Stage:	DO: Crediting
Grade Level:	Pre-K–1
GL Objective:	Crediting and Citing
Subject Area:	Social Studies
Unit Focus:	Communities

Figure 6.10 Early Elementary—DO—Crediting/Citing Lesson in Context

Subject Area Lesson Goal:

1. To learn why and how to credit.

2. To learn to use crediting/citing tools—Super3 Sam citing stickers.

Learning Activity:

- Class discussion: Why do we credit/cite? To give credit because the "source" deserves it. Also, to back up (support) what we say.

- When possible, give credit in our work and also at the end.

- Use "Super3 Citing Stickers" (or rubber stamps of similar images or make your own images) to give credit to "people, myself, computer, or books" (see Figure 6.11).

Figure 6.11 Super3™ Sam Citing Stickers

Assessment:

- Evidence: Observation of discussion; worksheet on what makes a community. On the worksheet, students circle pictures or write a word in the blank and then use the appropriate sticker to indicate where they got their information.
- Criteria: Understanding of "why." Accuracy in using stickers.

Big6™ Stage:	Use of Information: 4.2 Extract
Grade Level:	9–12
GL Objective:	Crediting and Citing
Subject Area:	Language Arts
Unit Focus:	Writing

Figure 6.12 Secondary Use of Information (4.2) Lesson in Context

Subject Area Lesson Goal:

1. To learn why, when, and how to cite.
2. To learn to use citing tools. (See Figure 6.12.)

Learning Activity:

- Class discussion: Why do we credit/cite? Enhances credibility, intellectual honesty. Discuss how it feels when you don't get credited or acknowledged.
- Complete and discuss "citation exercise" (e.g., Purdue OWL exercise, http://owl.english.purdue.edu/owl/resource/589/04/).
- Introduce recommended citation tool and approach.

Assessment:

- Evidence: Observation of discussion; citation exercise; citation tool screenshot or printout.
- Criteria: Understanding of "why." Accuracy on exercise. Success in using tool.

Help students decide when a citation is necessary by referring to the flowchart in Figure 6.13.

Again, technology offers us an easy alternative to the tedious compilation of a bibliography. Citation Machine (http://citationmachine.net/index2.php) is one interactive online citation generator that allows students to compile their citations in the standard format required by their school: MLA, APA, Turabian, or Chicago style. EasyBib (http://www.easybib.com/) is another automated bibliography and citation maker.

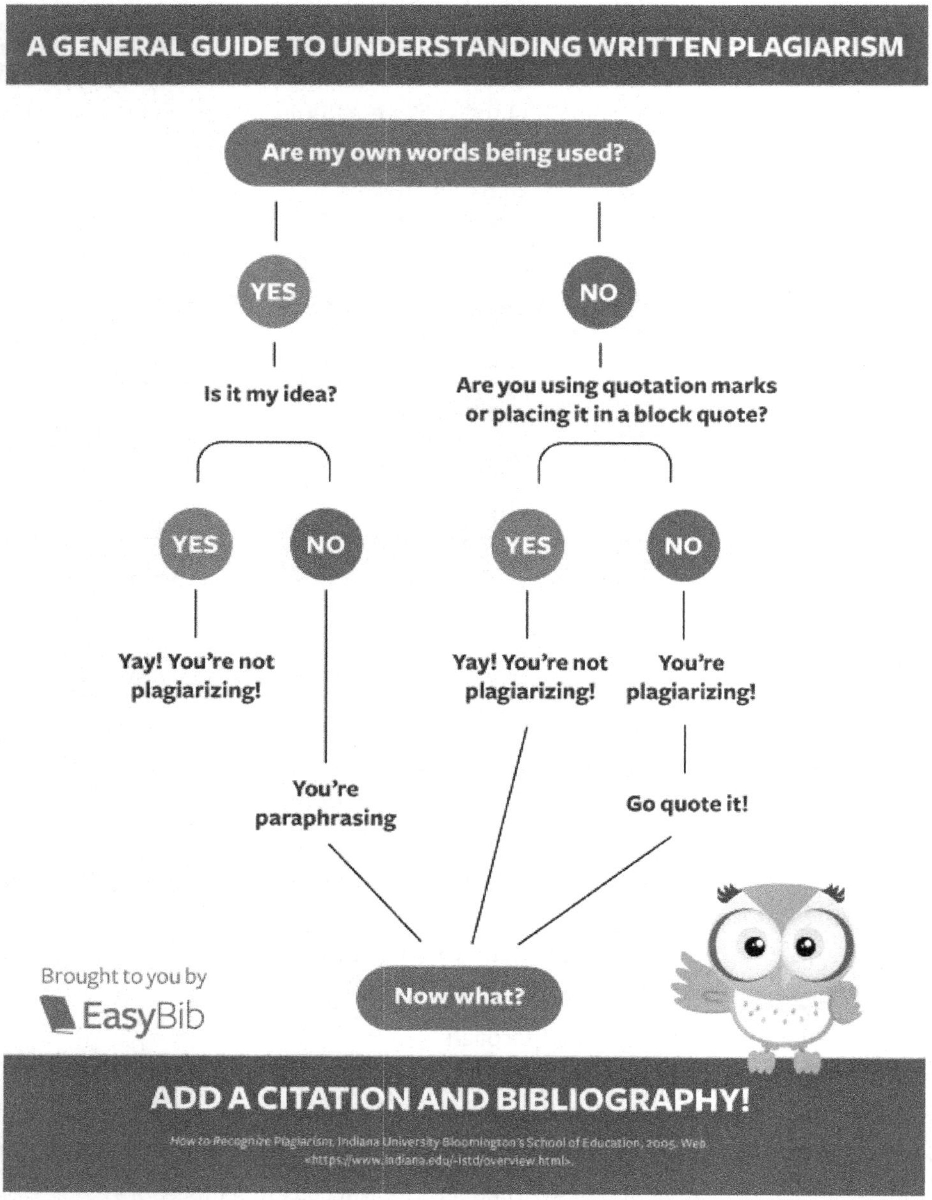

A GENERAL GUIDE TO UNDERSTANDING WRITTEN PLAGIARISM

Are my own words being used?

YES → Is it my idea?
- YES → Yay! You're not plagiarizing!
- NO → You're paraphrasing

NO → Are you using quotation marks or placing it in a block quote?
- YES → Yay! You're not plagiarizing!
- NO → You're plagiarizing! → Go quote it!

Brought to you by EasyBib

Now what?

ADD A CITATION AND BIBLIOGRAPHY!

How to Recognize Plagiarism, Indiana University Bloomington's School of Education, 2005. Web. <https://www.indiana.edu/~istd/overview.html>.

EasyBib (http://easybib.com/)

Figure 6.13 A General Guide to Understanding Written Plagiarism

Measured

Students need to know whether or not they have achieved the desired information literacy goals and objectives. Create *criteria* based on the learning objectives to clearly indicate the path to success. Criteria often reflect degrees of completeness, accuracy, and frequency of display. The language in a performance description should be specific to the grade level and readily accessible to students and parents. Figure 6.14 is a summary table of assessment criteria that might be applied to the Use of Information lessons above.

Colet Bartow created sample performance descriptors to distinguish among novice, nearing proficient, proficient, and advanced students learning note-taking skills. For fourth graders, the descriptors in Figure 6.15 apply to taking notes (Big6 stage 4.2).

Older students are more sophisticated in their note-taking strategies, but variations in quality of performance can still be identified in Figure 6.16.

Grade Level	Specific GLO	Big6™ Stage	Subject Area	Assignment	Evidence	Criteria
4	Take notes using digital tools	4.2	Science	Types of animals	Completed PowerPoint slides	Completeness, accuracy, sources
10–12	Paraphrase for note taking	4.1 4.2	Language arts or writing	Paraphrasing for note taking	Discussion notes, sample paraphrased selections	Accuracy, completeness
9–12	Credit and cite sources	4.2	Language arts or writing	Citation exercise	Observation of discussion, citation exercise, online citation tool	Understanding "why" to cite; accuracy on citation exercise; correct use of citation tool

Big6 by the Month: Use of Information (2012). Developed by Colet Bartow.

Figure 6.14 Assessment Criteria for Use of Information Lessons

Novice	Nearing Proficient	Proficient	Advanced
Omits most details, facts, or concepts when compiling information, and/or includes many irrelevant details.	Omits some details, facts, or concepts when compiling information, and/or includes some irrelevant details.	Compiles information (note taking, graphic organizers, etc.).	Gleans new insight from details, facts, and concepts when compiling information.
Novice	**Nearing Proficient**	**Proficient**	**Advanced**
All notes do not reflect a creative use of words and are not written using 4th-grade language and vocabulary. Rubistar rubric ID: 1641653	Most notes do not reflect a creative use of words and are not written using 4th-grade language and vocabulary.	Most notes reflect a creative use of words and are written using 4th-grade language and vocabulary.	All notes reflect a creative use of words and are written using 4th-grade or more advanced language and vocabulary.

Big6 by the Month: Use of Information (2012). Developed by Colet Bartow.

Figure 6.15 Sample Performance Descriptors for Note Taking (Grade 4)

Grade 8			
Novice	**Nearing Proficient**	**Proficient**	**Advanced**
Rely on single mode (read or listen or view) to extract information from resources provided.	Read, listen, and view as appropriate to accomplish task.	Read, listen, and view with purpose to accomplish task.	Read, listen, and view multiple resources with purpose to accomplish task.
Rely on one method of restating information.	Accurately restate information according to a model.	Recognize the differences among summarizing, paraphrasing, and/or directly quoting.	Accurately paraphrase, summarize, and quote information.
Grades 10–12			
Inconsistently make inferences from what is read, viewed, or heard.	Read, view, and listen to make inferences.	Consistently make inferences from what is read, viewed, or heard.	Formulate in-depth inferences from what is read, viewed, or heard.
Inconsistently summarize, paraphrase, and/or directly quote facts and details relevant to the question.	Occasionally summarize, paraphrase, and/or directly quote facts and details relevant to the question.	Summarize, paraphrase, and/or directly quote facts and details relevant to the question.	Consistently summarize, paraphrase, and/or directly quote facts and details relevant to the question.

Big6 by the Month: Use of Information (2012). Developed by Colet Bartow.

Figure 6.16 Sample Performance Descriptors for Note Taking (Grades 8–12)

Reported

Using a rubric to give a student feedback on an assignment is more informative and more accurate than a simple letter grade. In Figure 6.17, each level of performance is clearly described in language that students and their parents can understand:

Reporting Rubric:

Traditional Grading: 8/12 points or 66%

Standards Based: NP-P

Does your school provide parental access to a student information system via the web or a mobile application? In systems that provide a view of assignment details, include Big6 stage and learning objectives and then tie them to a monthly newsletter or other messaging system. Provide guided questions for discussion, as in Figure 6.18.

Skill	Novice (1)	Nearing Proficient (2)	Proficient (3)	Advanced (4)
Summarizing	Has great difficulty summarizing the article.	Summarizes most of the source accurately, but has some slight misunderstanding.	Uses several sentences to accurately describe what the source is about.	Uses 1–3 sentences to clearly describe what source is about.
Paraphrasing	Few big ideas included.	Some big ideas included.	Majority of big ideas included.	All big ideas included.
Quoting	No quotation marks or sources cited.	Quotation marks or source not included.	Quotation marks and source named.	Quotation marks included; source named and cited.

Big6 by the Month: Use of Information (2012). Developed by Colet Bartow.

Figure 6.17 Reporting Rubric for Note Taking

Sample Message for January	11th-grade students will be able to:	Questions to ask:
Dear Parents/Guardians: During the month of January, your student will work on a variety of projects and assignments. As part of each project, we will focus on stage 4 of the Big6 information problem-solving model: Use of Information. You can help reinforce these skills when you ask your student questions that relate to: 4.1 Engage information 4.2 Extract information The chart in this message details the skills students will practice and some questions you can ask to help students be successful as they complete assignments and projects. Please contact me if you have any questions. Sincerely, [provide contact information]	Engage with information by reading, viewing, or listening.	What are the main ideas that you read/saw/heard? How do the main ideas help you solve the problem or complete the assignment?
	Use specific strategies to effectively extract information from a variety of sources, regardless of format.	What's your favorite note-taking strategy? What's the difference among summarizing, paraphrasing, and using a quotation? How will you cite your sources? Why is it important to cite your sources for this assignment?

Big6 by the Month: Use of Information (2013). Developed by Colet Bartow.

Figure 6.18 Sample Report to Parents, Use of Information

Summary

The Big6 by the Month program emphasizes Use of Information skills in the month of January. We recommend targeting ICT literacy and Common Core standards by *defining* power grade level objectives that emphasize comprehension skills related to reading for purpose, identifying relevant information, extracting the information by taking notes (including summarizing, paraphrasing, and quoting), and citing sources in an established format. Then, create lesson plans in conjunction with local content assignments to help students accomplish each of the grade level power objectives.

The program is *predictable* because the entire school is focusing on developing Use of Information skills, and objectives, assignments, and lessons are also *predictable* if you use consistent approaches and formats. Create lesson plans in conjunction with local content assignments to help students achieve each of the grade level power objectives.

Measurement is integrated into schoolwork and assignments because you can identify evidence and criteria that demonstrate student performance on Use of Information skills.

And we urge you to continue or even expand your *reporting* mechanisms so that the ICT literacy program (aka Big6 or Super3 by the Month) is highly visible and understood by all students, teachers, administrators, parents, and decision makers. Effective reporting helps students to recognize the importance and usefulness of Use of Information skills and parents to become involved in reinforcing learned skills. Reporting also keeps the program front and center with teaching and administrative staff on the building or district level.

Online Resources

Useful Sites: Taking Notes

"Reading for Information: The Trash 'n' Treasure Method of Teaching Notetaking," by Barbara Jansen, http://www.big6.com/media/Jansen.ReadingforInformationTTnotetakingjansen.pdf

"PowerPoint for Note-taking Template," by Mike Eisenberg, http://big6.com/media/freestuff/Big6-Blank-Notetaking-Template.ppt

PowerPoint for Note-taking (You Tube video), by Mike Eisenberg, http://youtu.be/2xnNGHWwkgk

"INFOcus: Use of Information," by Ru Story-Huffman, http://big6.com/pages/lessons/articles/infocus-use-of-information.php

"Electronic Notetaking Template," by Janet Murray, http://janetsinfo.com/notesnew.doc

Graphic organizers, http://www.graphic.org/goindex.html

"Note Taking Tools" at Study2Learn wiki, http://study2learn.wikispaces.com/Note+Taking+Tools

Teach students to distinguish among "quoting, paraphrasing and summarizing," from Purdue University, https://owl.english.purdue.edu/owl/resource/563/01/

Paraphrase Exercises from the Purdue Online Writing Lab, http://owl.english.purdue.edu/owl/resource/619/1/

"Listen and Write" offers practice sessions in taking notes from audio and video files, http://www.listen-and-write.com/

Useful Sites: Citing Sources

"Citing and Crediting—Super3 Style," by Mike Eisenberg, http://big6.com/pages/lessons/articles/citing---for-the-very-young-super3-style.php

"Using the Big6 to Prevent Plagiarism," by Ru Story-Huffman, http://big6.com/pages/lessons/articles/using-the-big6-to-prevent-plagiarism.php

"Safe Practices: An Exercise," from the Purdue Online Writing Lab, http://owl.english.purdue.edu/owl/resource/589/04/

Chapter 7

"WE LEARN FROM OUR MISTAKES"

February:
Revisit and Reflect

In This Chapter

- ❏ Introduction: Progress to Date
- ❏ Defined: Big6™ by the Month Program, Standards, Grade Level Objectives
- ❏ Predictable: Schedule and Program Plan, Lesson Ideas
- ❏ Measured: Performance Descriptors, TRAILS Interim Assessment, Revisit and Reflect with Students
- ❏ Reported: Audience, Format
- ❏ Summary
- ❏ Online Resources

Introduction: Progress to Date

For the Big6 by the Month program in February, we recommend scheduling time and activities to reflect on the program to date, to make adjustments for the rest of the year, and to fill in gaps or go back and work on areas that would benefit from additional instruction. As part of this reflection and review, we encourage you to ask questions about all four elements of the program (defined, predictable, measured, and reported):

- What parts of the Big6 by the Month program are working well?
- What parts could be improved?
- What roadblocks, if any, have you encountered?
- What opportunities or boosts have you experienced?

Also, at this time of year many schools prepare for statewide testing, often held in March or April. Therefore, February is a good time to focus on how the Big6 Skills can improve student performance on standardized tests. For example, you may wish to revisit Chapter 6, Figure 6.9, for ideas about how to apply Big6 stage 4, Use of Information skills, to reading comprehension portions of statewide exams.

Defined

Standards

The Big6 by the Month program anchors instruction to standards. By February, we have identified relevant and priority information and communication technology (ICT) literacy standards from various sources, including AASL, ACRL, ISTE, and TRAILS. Here we ask the following:

- How has identifying ICT literacy standards helped focus Super3 or Big6 instruction each month?

- How useful are the various sources of standards? Are some more appropriate and useful for your school or district?

- Are there gaps or areas that need further development?

Content standards provide an essential link to subject area curriculum. By using the Common Core State Standards (or equivalent in states or countries that don't use the Common Core), we seek to identify power grade level objectives related to each of the Big6 stages. Here too we ask the following:

- How has identifying relevant Common Core or equivalent content standards helped focus Super3 or Big6 instruction?

- How useful are the Common Core or equivalent standards?

- Are there gaps or areas that need further development?

Grade Level Objectives

Standards provide a conceptual foundation for the Big6 by the Month program and goals to achieve. It is our task to make these standards meaningful—to operationalize the standards by identifying and defining *grade level objectives* or *learning expectations*. To make this practical and attainable, we divide the ICT literacy instructional program into manageable, month-by-month plans. In previous chapters, we provided examples from Montana's *Essential Learning Expectations for Information Literacy*. In February, helpful questions to ask include the following:

- How does selecting "power" grade level objectives help focus your information literacy instruction?

- Is your program comprehensive—that is, have you been able to plan objectives or learning expectations for every grade level in the school?

- Are there gaps or areas that need further development?

Predictable

The Big6 by the Month program is *predictable* because each month is devoted to a particular stage of the Big6 Skills.

Schedule and Program Plan

If you are responsible for ICT literacy instruction in your school, February is a good time to review the successes and challenges of the September through January effort:

- How well does using a monthly program structure help to deliver a comprehensive ICT literacy program?

- Is your information literacy instructional program reaching every student in your school?

- How could you adjust or adapt the schedule to make it more effective and efficient in your school?

- How well did the *Program Plan Template* help organize your instruction?
- To what extent do you manage information literacy instruction rather than directly delivering it? Is this balance working satisfactorily, or are adjustments needed?

Lesson Ideas

We have presented Super3 and Big6 lessons in context (i.e., tied to standards and subject areas) in each month using a predictable, standard format that identified standards and grade level objectives related to a Big6 stage, the grade level, the content area and lesson focus, the learning activity, and assessment evidence and criteria. (See the *Lesson Plan Template* in the "Templates" section of the appendices, or online at https://sites.google.com/site/big6xthemonth/file-cabinet.) Previous chapters included many lesson plans, summarized in Figure 7.1.

For February, as part of revisiting and reflecting, consider the following questions and make adjustments accordingly:

- How well does the lesson plan format help you connect standards and grade level objectives to individual lessons on Big6 stages?
- How easy is it to adapt and use the lessons provided?
- Are there gaps or areas that need further development?

Measured

Students need to know whether or not they have achieved the desired ICT literacy goals and objectives. Accurate assessment requires collecting evidence and applying specific criteria to the evidence.

Performance Descriptors

Performance descriptors distinguish between levels of achievement related to the criteria.

- What forms of evidence are most valuable for assessing student ICT literacy performance?
- What criteria did you apply to the evidence?
- Were you able to create performance descriptors to distinguish between levels of achievement?
- How well have students met the criteria established for learning objectives?

TRAILS Interim Assessment

While pausing for reflection in February and to measure student performance, you might consider administering a TRAILS test as an interim assessment:

- Do the results of the TRAILS assessments indicate that students have made progress in acquiring information literacy skills?
- What does TRAILS not include that we should consider?

Revisit and Reflect with Students

It is also valuable to use February to revisit and reflect with students about the Super3 or Big6 and their performance:

- Are students familiar and comfortable with the overall information problem-solving process: the Super3 and/or Big6?
- Which stages seem easy, and which are more difficult?

Big6™ Stage	Grade	Subject	Big6™/Super3™ Lesson	Assessment
PLAN	Pre-K, K	Science	Choose picture format	Choice and explanation
TD 1.1—Listen and retell the problem or task	2–4	Science	KWL (Know, Want to Know, Learn) chart related to cloud types. For W—create a Task Definition statement	Class responses, ease of completing
TD 1.1—Identify and define keywords	7–10	Math	Keywords in math story problems	Quiz on keywords Accuracy
TD 1.2—Understand the nature and kinds of info needed	4–6	Social Studies	Groups create a "bubble map" graphic organizer listing ALL the types of information they may possibly use.	Bubble map—quantity and quality of types of info
TD 1.2—Types of information	11–12	Social Studies	Big6 1.2 checklists	Complete, insightful
PLAN (Sources)	Pre-K, K	Science	Choose from two possible sources	Able to choose and explain
PLAN (Game)	K–2	All	Identify information sources	Group performance—accurate, appropriate, realistic
ISS 2.1—Brainstorm possible sources	2	Science	Generate Post-it notes of possible sources	Post-its—expect three per student
ISS 2.2— Select the best sources	9–10	Social Studies	From brainstormed list, select the best and explain why—relevance and credibility	Justifications
DO	K–1	Science	Understand browse, search	Worksheet—preferences
L&A 3.1—Locate all sources	7–8	Health	Locate multiple resources using search tools	Essay
L&A 3.2—Text features of books	1–2	Reading	Use parts of a book to define vocabulary words	Worksheet
U of I 4.2—Note-taking—PowerPoint and other tools	4–8	Science	Use PPT for taking notes	Completed PPT slides
U of I 4.1/ 4.2— Quoting, paraphrasing, summarizing	10–12	English	Ohio U on differences among quoting, paraphrasing, and summarizing/Purdue practice materials	Samples and work—accuracy and appropriateness
DO	Pre-K–1	Social Studies	Crediting—Citing	Super3 Sam Citing Stickers
U of I 4.2—Crediting and citing sources	9–12	English—Writing	Purdue OWL exercise	Citation exercise—accuracy

Figure 7.1 Summary of Lessons: Task Definition (PLAN) through Use of Information (DO)

- Consider each Super3 or Big6 Stage:
  - For PLAN and DO, what works well, and what are the challenges?
  - For Task Definition, are students able to dissect an assignment and plan for completion?
  - In Information Seeking Strategies, what are preferred sources, and why?
  - Do you have any special Location & Access (i.e., search) tips to share?
  - For Use of Information, what note-taking approaches do you use?

Also ask students to revisit and reflect on their assignments in terms of overall performance and skills on specific stages:

- What worked well?
- Where did you encounter problems?
- Do you need more help, and if so, with what?

Reported

Audience

Since the primary activity in February is to revisit and reflect, this is a good time to provide a preliminary report about the overall program and student performance. Options include a short report to faculty (perhaps verbally at a meeting or in a one- or two-page electronic or print report) as well as a more extensive report to building administrators and decision-making bodies. The aggregated results of the TRAILS interim assessment can also be shared with teachers and school leaders. Parents and students should also be apprised of how well the program is going, as well as issues or challenges.

Format

Informal reporting is also recommended: through conversations, e-mail, online social networks, and comments at meetings. We encourage you to refer often to the ICT literacy program and regularly emphasize what the students are learning as part of the defined, predictable, measured, and reported, comprehensive Big6 by the Month program.

In reflecting on the effectiveness of the program and your performance, consider these questions:

- To what audiences did you report?
- What formats did you use?
- How receptive were the audiences? Do they have special concerns or issues?
- How were the reports used by the various audiences? For example, did parents engage in the follow-up activities that were listed in the monthly reports?

Summary

The Big6 by the Month program schedules February to revisit the program and reflect on what's working and what needs improvement. From a management perspective, February provides time for analysis, revision, and planning. From an instructional perspective, we can use February to reinforce key ideas, fill in gaps, and interact with students and teachers about the ICT literacy program.

This chapter offers specific actions and questions for reviewing your implementation of the four elements of the program and reflecting on your progress so far. Working within the Big6 by the Month program structure, you should be comfortable with defining grade level objectives based on ICT literacy and Common Core standards and with offering predictable schedules and formats for planning both the program and individual lessons. Assessment depends on clear identification of the *evidence* and *criteria* by which students will be assessed. Reports in a variety of formats should be delivered to all appropriate audiences. Use the questions in each section to guide your reflections.

Online Resources

"Evaluating Big6 Units," by Barbara Jansen, http://big6.com/media/freestuff/Evaluating_Big6_Units.pdf

"Super3 Action Research Report—Blending Super3 with Math and Writing: One Teacher's Quest for Learning (Grade 3), eNewsletter 10.4, 1," by Teresa Waters, http://big6.com/pages/about/research/super3-action-research-report.php

"The Big Six Information Skills as a Metacognitive Scaffold," by Sara Wolf, http://www.ala.org/aasl/sites/ala.org.aasl/files/content/aaslpubsandjournals/slr/vol6/SLMR_BigSixInfoSkills_V6.pdf

"The Big6 Works: Empirical Evidence from One Middle School's Experience, Big6 eNewsletter, 11.2.1," by Dr. Emily S. Harris, http://big6.com/pages/about/research/the-big6-works.php

Chapter 8

"THE WHOLE IS GREATER THAN THE SUM OF ITS PARTS"

March:
Synthesis

5.1 Organize information from multiple sources.

5.2 Present the information.

In This Chapter

❑ Introduction: Synthesis

❑ Defined: Standards and Grade Level Objectives

❑ Predictable: Lesson Ideas

❑ Measured: Student Self-Assessment, Performance Descriptors

❑ Reported: Student Self-Assessment, Standards-Based Reports

❑ Summary

❑ Online Resources

Introduction: Synthesis

Big6 stage 5, Synthesis, is the culminating stage of the information problem-solving process. Synthesis involves organizing, comparing, combining, processing, and finally presenting information. Synthesis brings it all together to finish the job. Sometimes Synthesis can be as simple as retelling a fact, writing short answers on homework worksheets, taking a test, or making a decision. At other times, Synthesis can be more complex and can involve the use of many sources, a variety of media or presentation formats, and effective communication of abstract ideas. Every subject area—particularly English or language arts—focuses on Synthesis.

5.0 Synthesis

5.1 Organize from multiple sources

5.2 Present the information

Synthesis involves determining the best ways to assemble, integrate, organize, and convey the information to meet the original task. In Synthesis 5.1, students pull all their information together, sort through and choose what to use, and organize the information to meet the task. In Synthesis 5.2, students decide how they are going to communicate through appropriate and effective products.

For Synthesis 5.1, students need to be able to fit all the various pieces of information together into a product, presentation, or even a decision. We like to ask two basic questions:

- What organizational options suit your students' assignments?
- Which presentation format options suit the assignment?

Examples of Synthesis 5.1 include students demonstrating the ability to do the following:

- Combine information from articles, notes, images, websites, books, and interviews about a current events issue.
- Put dates and events in the right order on a timeline.
- Organize pictures so that they tell a story.
- Represent a setting or event in a diorama.
- Use software for word processing, presentation (e.g., PowerPoint) or note taking to arrange information.

For Synthesis 5.2, students should consider options and actions for presenting and then design and deliver the presentation. Here are some relevant questions to consider:

- What choices are available (e.g., written, graphic, verbal, multimedia, online)?
- Which approach is most appropriate and feasible for the task at hand?
- What digital tools—software, online systems, apps—are available to help create and present information?

Many digital tools are aimed at improving design, presentation, and production, including the following:

- Word processing
- Desktop publishing
- Graphics and photo editing
- Audio and video editing
- Presentation software (e.g., PowerPoint)
- Animation
- Website creation
- E-mail
- Social media (e.g., Twitter, Facebook, Instagram)
- Electronic spreadsheets
- Databases
- Graphic organizers

Synthesis includes creating products or presentations of any kind—even computer programs, games, or apps. Encourage students to think creatively and select options that will work best for their situation. Teaching staff should consider the types of digital tools that students should master. Consider at what grade level mastery is appropriate, and plan these expectations as part of defining grade level objectives, which we explain in the next section.

Writing remains the most used and important presentation approach. Students need to continually improve their composition and writing skills in a variety of situations and formats, including essays, lab reports, reflective paragraphs, research papers, and abstracts. Teachers at all levels still complain that "students just can't write" in spite of having received almost daily instruction in writing since early elementary school grades. This reflects both the complexity of communicating through writing as well as its importance. The information and communication technology (ICT) literacy program can help by working closely with the English and language arts program and teachers.

Examples of Synthesis 5.2 skills include students demonstrating the ability to do the following:

- Use graphics in a speech.
- Represent a still life in different media.
- Write an essay on a standardized test.
- Post reactions to current issues using social media.
- Use PowerPoint to create stand-alone slide shows.
- Draw and label a map of Africa.
- Write a computer program that involves graphics.
- Use electronic spreadsheets or other tools to graph data collected during a science experiment.
- Properly cite online sources.

Defined

Complementing existing instruction in writing and other forms of communication, the ICT literacy program focuses on **Synthesis** for the month of March. Once students have extracted the relevant and credible information that they will need to complete an assignment, they turn to organizing it to create a presentation or product that effectively communicates the results of their research. The Big6 by the Month program *defines* each stage of the Big6 in terms of standards augmented by grade level objectives or learning expectations.

Standards for Synthesis

Each of these sets of ICT literacy standards emphasizes the importance of *analyzing* and *organizing* information as well as *creating* a product that effectively communicates with others. (See Figure 8.1.)

ICT Literacy Standards Related to Synthesis	
AASL	2.1.4 Use technology and other information tools to **analyze** and **organize** information. 3.1.4 Use technology and other information tools to **organize** and **display** knowledge and understanding in ways that others can view, use, and assess.
ACRL	3.3 **Synthesizes** main ideas to construct new concepts. 4.1 Applies new and prior information to the planning and creation of a particular **product** or performance. 4.3 Communicates the **product** or performance effectively to others.
NETS-S	2a. Interact, collaborate, and **publish** with peers, experts, or others employing a variety of digital environments and media. 2b. **Communicate** information and ideas effectively to multiple audiences using a variety of media and formats.

Compiled by Janet Murray from *AASL Standards for the 21st-Century Learner,* © 2007, American Association of School Librarians, http://www.ala.org/aasl/standards; Association of College and Research Libraries, "Information Literacy Competency Standards for Higher Education," © 2000, http://www.ala.org/ala/mgrps/divs/acrl/standards/informationliteracycompetency.cfm; and ISTE, National Educational Technology Standards (NETS-S) for Students.

Figure 8.1 ICT Literacy Standards Related to Synthesis

When we teach students how to apply the information they have located and chosen as relevant for an assignment, it is critically important to focus on both aspects of these standards: *organizing* and *presenting information*.

The ICT literacy program emphasizes that writing and communication skills are important in all areas of the curriculum, not just as part of English, language arts, or research. The Common Core State Standards are particularly well-developed and valuable in the Synthesis area, defining what every high school graduate must know and be able to do in order to succeed in entry-level college courses or the workplace. Many of these standards pertain directly to both substages of Synthesis (see Figure 8.2).

When students synthesize the information they have gathered and organized, they show us what they have learned. In the Common Core standards, there are references to **presenting**, **producing**, and **publishing**. Student-created products should reflect **evidence** and **reasoning** and should clearly address **purpose** and **audience**. "Mathematical Practices" refers to precise **communication**.

There are many more Common Core Standards related to Synthesis than any other Big6 stage, but the Big6 offers us a **process** to help students achieve these Synthesis standards: student products will significantly improve when the students clearly understand the task or assignment, carefully locate relevant information, evaluate their sources of information for credibility, and take adequate notes. We can improve students' performance when we provide them with the information literacy skills that are necessary to be successful.

Examine your state's content standards to find similar wording. (Use the *Standards Template* in the "Templates" section of the appendices.)

Related Common Core Standards	5.1 Organize information
Reading	8. Delineate and evaluate the argument and specific claims in a text, including the validity of the **reasoning** as well as the relevance and sufficiency of the **evidence.**
Reading: Informational Text	1. Cite textual **evidence** to support analysis of what the text says explicitly as well as inferences drawn from the text.
Reading: Science and Technical Subjects	9. **Compare** and contrast the information gained from experiments, simulations, video, or multimedia sources with that gained from reading a text on the same topic.
Writing	2. Write informative/explanatory texts to examine and convey complex ideas and information clearly and accurately through the effective **selection**, **organization**, and **analysis** of content. 9. Draw **evidence** from literary or informational texts to support analysis, reflection, and research.
Mathematical Practices	1. Make sense of problems and persevere in solving them: . . . explain **correspondences** among equations, verbal descriptions, tables, and graphs.

Related Common Core Standards	5.2 Present information
Reading	7. **Integrate** and evaluate content presented in diverse media and formats, including visually and quantitatively, as well as in words.
Reading: Informational Text	7. **Integrate** information presented in different media or formats (e.g., visually, quantitatively) as well as in words to develop a coherent understanding of a topic or issue.
Reading: History and Social Studies	7. **Integrate** visual information (e.g., in charts, graphs, photographs, videos, or maps) with other information in print and digital texts.
Writing	1. Write arguments to support claims in an analysis of substantive topics or texts, using valid **reasoning** and relevant and sufficient **evidence**. 4. **Produce** clear and coherent writing in which the development, organization, and style are appropriate to **task**, **purpose**, and **audience**. 6. Use technology, including the Internet, to **produce** and **publish** writing and to interact and collaborate with others.
Speaking and Listening	4. **Present** information, findings, and supporting **evidence** such that listeners can follow the line of **reasoning** and the organization, development, and style are appropriate to **task**, **purpose**, and **audience**.
Mathematical Practices	3. Construct viable arguments: . . . justify conclusions. 6. Attend to precision: . . . **communicate** precisely to others.

Compiled by Janet Murray and Colet Bartow from The Common Core State Standards Initiative, http://www.corestandards.org /the-standards. See "Big6™ Skills Aligned with Common Core Standards," http://janetsinfo.com/Big6_CCSSIStds.htm.

Figure 8.2 Common Core Standards Related to Synthesis

Grade Level Objectives

For each Big6 or Super3 stage, our goal as teachers, technology teachers, or teacher-librarians is to identify "power" information literacy goals and learning objectives for all students in our school. These goals and objectives should link to relevant national or local learning standards. Figure 8.3 displays Montana's *Essential Learning Expectations for Information Literacy* related to Synthesis. Notice the progression of skills and the emphasis on organizing information from multiple resources as well as the references to citing sources.

Use the *Grade Level Objectives Template* in the "Templates" section of the appendices to create learning expectations for each grade level at your school.

Cross-Grade Objective	Grades					
	K	1	2	3	4	5
2.5 *Organize* information to solve problems.	A. Sequence information.	A. Sequence and sort information.	A. Organize information.	A. Organize information.	A. Organize and select relevant information.	A. Transfer information into a prescribed format to accomplish task.
2.6 *Create* a product that presents findings.	A. Design original work following established guidelines.	A. Design original work following established guidelines.	A. Design original work following established guidelines.	A. Design original work following established guidelines.	A. Design original work following established guidelines.	A. Identify audience. B. Construct an original product that meets task criteria.
4.2 Identify the owner of ideas and information: *cite sources.*	C. Credit sources.	C. Credit sources.	B. Credit sources.	C. Cite sources.	B. Credit sources.	C. Credit the intellectual property of others.

Cross-Grade Objective	Grades				
	6	7	8	9–10	11–12
2.5 BM 8 *Organize* and manage information.	A. Transfer information into a prescribed format to accomplish task.	A. Arrange information into a format to accomplish task.	A. Arrange information into a format to accomplish task.	A. Sort and categorize gathered information. B. Review and refine the gathered information.	A. Sort and categorize gathered information. B. Review and refine the gathered information.
2.6 Create a product that presents findings: *audience.*	A. Identify audience. B. Construct an original product that meets task criteria.	A. Construct a product that meets task criteria and is audience appropriate.	A. Design and create an original product appropriate to task criteria and audience.	A. Choose the appropriate medium for presentation based on audience.	A. Choose the appropriate medium for presentation based on audience.
2.6 Create a product that presents findings: *format.*	C. Present final product in assigned format.	B. Present final product in appropriate format.	B. Present final product in appropriate format.	B. Create original product. D. Present and defend the product.	B. Create original product. D. Present and defend the product.
4.2 BM 8 Appropriately *credits* ideas and works of others.	C. Credit the intellectual property of others.	C. Credit the intellectual property of others.	D. Credit the intellectual property of others.	D. Credit the intellectual property of others.	D. Credit the intellectual property of others.

Compiled by Janet Murray from Montana's *Essential Learning Expectations for Information Literacy,* http://www.opi.mt.gov/pdf /Standards/10FebELE_LibMedia.xls.

BM = benchmark

Figure 8.3 Grade Level Objectives Related to Synthesis

Predictable

By March, the *predictable* Big6 by the Month program should be well-established and recognized in your school or district. You should now be familiar with developing an overall instructional plan and specific lesson plans for the month's program, that is, plans customized to your school's unique calendar, organization, and schedule that focus on Synthesis instruction and learning in March. As before, you will want to integrate ICT instruction with the subject area classroom curriculum by identifying one or two major assignments for each grade and teacher and then developing Synthesis lessons targeted to classroom assignments or units.

Lesson Ideas for Synthesis

Due to the extensiveness of lesson and instructional options for Synthesis, we depart from offering a number of specific lessons and instead offer more generalizable techniques and approaches that can be adapted for any grade level. You can then develop your own lessons using the *Lesson Plan Template*. We do provide one sample lesson to demonstrate how we move from technique to subject area–integrated lesson.

Big6™ Substage 5.1: Organizing Information

The first step in Synthesis—creating a final product—is being able to organize the information collected from multiple sources: Big6 stage 5.1. After students have selected information resources and taken notes with the purpose of the assignment firmly in mind, they should be ready to determine the best ways to organize the information.

Students are given a PowerPoint slide set and asked to reorganize the slides in a PowerPoint presentation in some way. Not only do the students learn organizational skills but they also review subject area content as well. For younger students learning the Super3, you can limit the number of slides and simply ask them to organize them in a logical, Super3 sequence: Beginning, Middle, and End. As the students improve their organizing skills, you can do follow-up lessons with more slides. You can also include slides that are not relevant or credible and require students to identify and delete irrelevant or noncredible slides. This same technique can be used with other presentation, note-taking, or graphic organizer systems such as Prezi (http://prezi.com/), Evernote (http://evernote.com/), or Kidspiration (http://www.inspiration.com/Kidspiration).

Figure 8.4 is a sample lesson that uses this PowerPoint slide set technique and builds on the "Taking Notes Using Digital Tools" lesson from January: Use of Information in Chapter 6 (see Figure 6.6). Again, while the specific lesson is targeted to grade 4, the underlying technique of the lesson is very flexible and can be used for K–12. For example, for upper elementary or secondary students, you can require them to organize the slides using alternative organizational schemes: organize by sequence, storyline, categories, timeline, even alphabetically. This activity helps them learn that the same information can be presented in different ways.

Big6™ Stage:	Synthesis: 5.1 Organize information
Grade Level:	4
GL Objective:	Organize notes using digital tools
Subject Area:	Science
Unit Focus:	Types of animals

Figure 8.4 Elementary Synthesis (5.1) Lesson in Context

Subject Area Lesson Goal: To become familiar with animal vocabulary and to provide an example for each animal type. VOCABULARY: invertebrates, arachnids, crustaceans, insects, mollusks, sponges, vertebrates, reptiles, amphibians, mammals.

Learning Activity:

1. Students will work in teams of three (3) to organize the information they have gathered on PowerPoint slides.
2. Students first practice using the sample PowerPoint slide set on turtles (see Figure 8.5).
3. After organizing the slides, the students will compare their results to the sample organized by categories (see Figure 8.6).

Assessment:

- Evidence: Completed PowerPoint slides.
- Criteria: (1) Able to use PowerPoint, reorder slides. (2) Logic—slides arranged in logical sequence. (3) Source—relevant and credible.

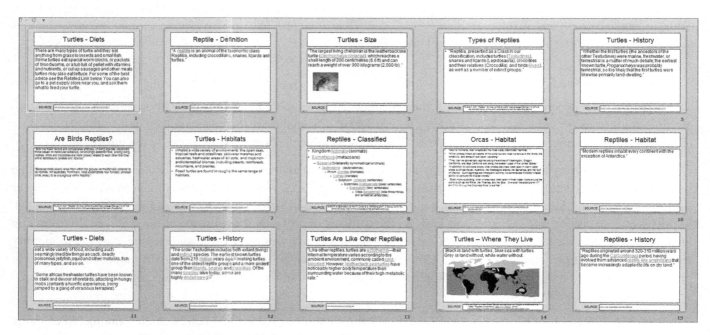

Figure 8.5 Sample PowerPoint Slide Set on Turtles: Unorganized

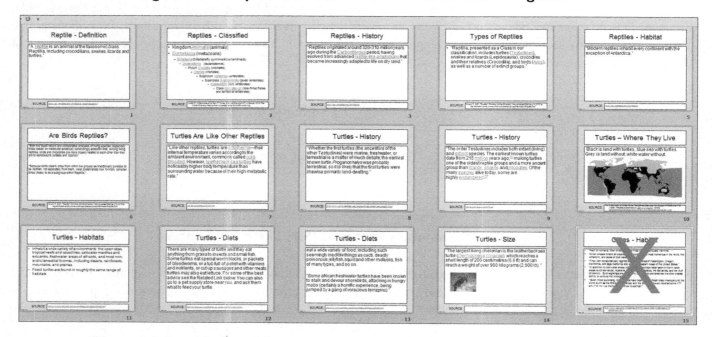

Figure 8.6 Sample PowerPoint Slide Set on Turtles: Reorganized by Categories

Big6 Substage 5.2: Present Information

In the "Grade Level Objectives" section above, notice the emphasis on considering the audience and purpose before choosing an appropriate format for a presentation. This is a very important understanding that we want to emphasize from the earliest grades through high school. There are many alternatives to research papers, some of which may actually better communicate the information as well as offer superior indicators of the extent of student learning.

A generalizable approach is to engage students to think about audience and purpose and then consider a wide range of options for presenting. For younger children, you may limit their presentation choices to just two or three (e.g., make a picture, fill out a worksheet, share verbally with the class). The key is to have them consider and be able to explain "why" they choose a certain option—in relation to audience and purpose. As students move up in grades, you can involve them more in brainstorming and analyzing alternatives as well as creating more complex and sophisticated presentations.

Figure 8.7 is a table of options that can be used with middle or upper grade students. Students can analyze the choices in the table as well as edit, change, and expand the table to include more 21st-century options.

For example, Kathy Schrock's "Bloomin' Apps" web page (http://www.schrockguide.net/bloomin-apps.html) is an excellent resource for identifying Android/Google, iPad/iPhone, and state-of-the art web applications in relation to Bloom's Revised Taxonomy. When students are applying and creating, they are doing Big6 stage 5, Synthesis. Students could even use a beginning coding program like Scratch, from MIT (http://scratch.mit.edu/), to create a game or application to present information. And notice that a graphic organizer might also be considered a final product as well as an organizational strategy.

Citing Sources

Another generalizable approach focuses on a major concern in education at all levels: citing sources and plagiarism. Mike Eisenberg prefers to talk about "giving credit to your sources" because it more accurately describes the reason for citing sources. Janet Murray asks students how they would *feel* if someone else submitted their carefully produced art project. She thinks students can understand feeling "bad, sad, mad" if someone "stole" their work; then we can ask them to relate to the feelings of the author or composer or programmer whose hard work deserves "credit."

Mary Thweatt (Dallas, Texas ISD), one of our previous Big6 by the Month webinar participants, described a creative lesson that makes the issues of crediting and citing very personal:

> I actually have my students draw a picture, write a poem, etc. and then turn them in unsigned. I then randomly hand them back out and tell students to sign the work they received if they like it. They then show/present the work they "plagiarized" as their own. Of course the real creator protests and we get a really dynamic conversation about feelings about someone else taking credit for their work.

Understanding the reasons for crediting sources is more important than learning a particular format for citations. We recommend creating a "culture of citing" to fight plagiarism by using the following methods:

- Model citing in teaching and presenting.

- Show "bad" examples—exaggerate plagiarism.

- Have students cite sources all the time.

- Expect citing in class discussions as well.

- Do not accept work without citing.

- Focus on citations in context more than bibliographies.

- Require "annotated" bibliographies, with annotations explaining "why" students selected a particular source as well as their "credibility" analysis of the source.

FORMS OF REPRESENTATION

TECHNOLOGY	DRAMATIC	THREE-DIMENSIONAL	VISUAL	VERBAL	GRAPHIC ORGANIZER
Multimedia presentations	Role play	Sculpture	Drawing	Interview	Concept map
Slide show	Tableau	Construction	Cartoon	Speech	Storyboard
Newscast	Play	Display	Diagram	Debate	Outline
Computer graphic	Dramatization	Diorama	Painting	Discussion	T chart
Video	Skit	Collage	Poster	Oral presentation	KWL chart
Recording*		Collection	Photograph	Poetry reading	Venn diagram
Commercials		Scrapbook	Postcard	Teach a lesson	Note taking
		Game	Map	Dialogue	Chart
		Model	Design	Song	Time line
				Reader's Theater	Graph
				Rap	Data table
					Grid/matrices

WRITTEN

NARRATIVE	EXPOSITORY	PERSONAL	PERSUASIVE	GUIDELINES
Stories	Research report	Personal letter	Persuasive writing	Rules
Essays	Magazine article	Journal	Editorial	Instructions
Character portrait	Newspaper article	Diary	Advertisement	
Script	Book report/review	Log	Letter to the editor	
Story endings	Biography	Autobiography	Proposal	
First person narrative	Business letter	Resume		

This table was created to support the AT&T/UCLA Initiative for the 21st Century Literacies. Forms of Representation was created by Sharon Sutton.

Reprinted with permission from Murray, *Achieving Educational Standards Using the Big6* (http://www.kn.pacbell.com/wired/21stcent /representation.html no longer available).

* Information updated to reflect technology change from Audiotape to Recording.

Figure 8.7 Forms of Representation and Presentation

Doug Johnson, Director of Technology in the Burnsville-Eagan-Savage (MN) Schools, identifies the characteristics of "low probability of plagiarism" projects, some of which are discussed here:

- "LPP projects give students choices." It makes sense that students are more motivated when they are exploring subjects they have chosen. Give them choices of product as well; some students will be able to display the results of their learning better in a format other than a research paper.

- "LPP projects stress higher level thinking skills and creativity." Students are much less likely to plagiarize if the assignment requires them to draw conclusions or support a hypothesis with the information they have gathered. That's why the Big6 by the Month program stresses asking essential questions in stage 1, Task Definition.

- "LPP projects can be complex, but are broken into manageable steps." That's **why** we use the Big6. ("Plagiarism-Proofing Assignments," by Doug Johnson, http://www.doug-johnson.com/dougwri/plagiarism-proofing-assignments.html)

If students have carefully recorded their sources of information while taking notes, compiling the list of sources in the format required by the assignment will be fairly straightforward. Again, technology offers us an easy alternative to the tedious compilation of a bibliography. Citation Machine (http://citationmachine.net) is one interactive online citation generator that allows students to compile their citations in the standard format required by their school: MLA, APA, Turabian, or Chicago. EasyBib (http://www.easybib.com/) is another automatic bibliography and citation maker. See the "Online Resources" at the end of this chapter for more examples.

Part of developing a comprehensive, predictable ICT literacy instructional program for March is to build on and expand student learning from year to year. This sequencing and scaffolding should be reflected in the grade level objectives and the lessons developed for each grade level.

Measured

Assessment strategies—particularly the evidence and criteria—should be carefully considered and determined *before* the assignment is given to students. This approach is sometimes called "backward design" and is detailed in Jay McTighe and Grant Wiggins's *Understanding by Design* (http://shop.ascd.org/Default.aspx?TabID=55&ProductId=406&Understanding-by-design-expanded-2nd-edition). A unit plan based on the backward design model contains the elements shown in Figure 8.8.

Unit Plan		
Desired Results	Big6 Stage 5, Synthesis	Content Standards
	Enduring Understandings	Essential Questions
Assessment Evidence	Performance Tasks	Content Assessment
	Information Skills Assessment/Performance Rubric	Content Evidence
Learning Plan	Lesson Progression	Materials and Resources
	Websites/Reference	Other Details

Big6 by the Month: Synthesis (2013). Designed by Colet Bartow.

Figure 8.8 Sample Unit Plan for Synthesis Based on Backward Design

Students need to know whether or not they have achieved the desired ICT literacy goals and objectives. The process of synthesizing the information students have collected presents an ideal opportunity for *formative assessment*. Students can engage in self-assessment before submitting their completed assignments, using the checklists in Figures 8.9 and 8.10. This will help students (and their teachers) identify areas that are incomplete or confusing as well as highlight the need for assistance or further instruction to complete the assignment successfully.

5.1 Organize from multiple sources

Criteria	Not Yet (0)	Yes (1)
I have used an appropriate organization strategy. Circle One: Sorting/Outline/Concept Map		
I have organized my information around topics and subtopics using my organization strategy.		
I have enough supporting evidence to answer/solve my information problem.		
I have included information from the required sources.		

Big6 by the Month: Synthesis (2012). Developed by Colet Bartow.

Figure 8.9 Self-Assessment for Synthesis 5.1

5.2 Present the information

Presentation Readiness Checklist	Not Yet (0)	Yes (1)
I have identified the audience.		
I have completed each of the assignment requirements:*		
Length: no more than 15 minutes		
Format: PowerPoint presentation/video		
Catchy Title: _____		
Transitions for each section		
Satisfying conclusion		
Source credits complete		

Big6 by the Month: Synthesis (2012). Developed by Colet Bartow.

*adapt criteria to reflect assignment requirements

Figure 8.10 Presentation Readiness Checklist

Students can self-assess their preparation to present the information. This differs from the summative evaluation that students will do in Big6 stage 6, Evaluation, when they will evaluate the final product and the process used to solve the information problem. A readiness checklist provides the opportunity for students to revisit their plan and make adjustments in order to successfully complete the task.

Performance Descriptors

Performance descriptors should incorporate *criteria* based on the learning objectives to clearly indicate the path to success. The criteria must reflect the standards and grade level objectives identified for the unit of study or project, and they should not be so extensive that students lose focus and the learning objectives become diluted. Criteria often reflect degrees of completeness, accuracy, and frequency of display. The language in a performance description should be specific to the grade level and readily accessible to students and parents.

Colet Bartow created sample performance descriptors to distinguish among novice, nearing proficient, proficient, and advanced student learning organization skills. See Figures 8.11 and 8.12.

Novice	Nearing Proficient	Proficient	Advanced
Inaccurately sort and categorize gathered information.	Sort and categorize gathered information with *some* accuracy.	*Accurately* sort and categorize gathered information.	*Sort, categorize, and prioritize* gathered information.
Infrequently review and refine the gathered information.	*Sometimes* review and refine the gathered information.	Review and refine the gathered information.	*Continually* review and refine the gathered information.

Big6 by the Month: Synthesis (2012). Developed by Colet Bartow.

Figure 8.11 Sample Performance Descriptors for Synthesis 5.1 (Grades 9–10)

Novice	Nearing Proficient	Proficient	Advanced
a. Choose the medium for presentation *regardless of audience*.	a. Choose the appropriate medium for presentation with *some consideration of audience*.	a. Choose the appropriate medium for presentation *based on audience*.	Choose a unique medium for presentation that *clearly considers audience*.
b. Create original product to meet *minimal* task requirements.	b. Create original product to meet *most* task requirements.	b. Create original product that meets *all* task requirements.	b. Create *high quality* original product that meets *all* task requirements.

Big6 by the Month: Synthesis (2012). Developed by Colet Bartow.

Figure 8.12 Sample Performance Descriptors for Synthesis 5.2 (Grades 9–10)

Reported

The student self-assessment checklists presented above can be easily adapted to give students the opportunity to "report" to themselves and their teachers. When students learn to realistically assess themselves, their teachers can expect their performance to improve on future assignments and projects. Figures 8.13 and 8.14 offer examples of using self-assessment checklists for self-reporting.

Organization Check-log	Not Yet (0)	Yes	Reflection
I have used an appropriate organization strategy. Circle one: Sorting/Outline/Concept Map			3 = I did a terrific job. 2 = I did a satisfactory job. I = I need to do much better.
I have organized my information around topics and subtopics using my organization strategy.			3 = I did a terrific job. 2 = I did a satisfactory job. I = I need to do much better.
I have enough supporting evidence to answer/solve my information problem.			3 = I did a terrific job. 2 = I did a satisfactory job. I = I need to do much better.
I have included information from the required sources.			3 = I did a terrific job. 2 = I did a satisfactory job. I = I need to do much better.

Big6 by the Month: Synthesis (2012). Developed by Colet Bartow.

Figure 8.13 Organization Check-log (Self-Assessment and Reporting)

Presentation Readiness Checklist	Not Yet (0)	Yes	Reflection
I have identified the audience.			3 = I did a terrific job. 2 = I did a satisfactory job. I = I need to do much better.
Format: PowerPoint presentation/video			3 = I did a terrific job. 2 = I did a satisfactory job. I = I need to do much better.
Transitions for each section			3 = I did a terrific job. 2 = I did a satisfactory job. I = I need to do much better.
Satisfying conclusion			3 = I did a terrific job. 2 = I did a satisfactory job. I = I need to do much better.
Source credits complete			3 = I did a terrific job. 2 = I did a satisfactory job. I = I need to do much better.

Big6 by the Month: Synthesis (2012). Developed by Colet Bartow.

Figure 8.14 Presentation Readiness Checklist (Self-Assessment and Reporting)

Parents can also encourage their children and help them in self-assessment and reporting. For example, a March report, letter, or newsletter home can explain how parents can become more involved (see Figure 8.15).

Sample Message for March: Dear Parents/Guardians: During the month of March, your student will work on a variety of projects and assignments. As part of each project, we will focus on stage 5 of the Big6 information problem-solving model: Synthesis. You can help reinforce these skills when you ask your student questions that relate to: 5.1 Organize from multiple sources. 5.2 Present the information. The chart in this message details the skills students will practice and some questions you can ask to help students be successful as they complete assignments and projects. Please contact me if you have any questions. Sincerely, [provide contact information]	9th-grade students will be able to:	Questions to ask:
	Efficiently organize information.	How did you organize your information? Does your assignment meet the requirements for organization and amount of information? Did you credit the sources that you actually used in the assignment?
	Create original written work, speeches, models, or other presentations.	What does your final project/ assignment look like? How long does it take to present? Do you have all of the materials you need to create the final project?

Big6 by the Month: Synthesis (2013). Developed by Colet Bartow.

Figure 8.15 Sample Report to Parents Regarding Synthesis and Self-Assessment

Standards-Based Reporting

The Big6 by the Month program *defines* each Big6 stage in terms of national ICT literacy and Common Core standards. We emphasize the use of performance descriptors and rubrics because they reflect student progress more clearly than simple letter grades. Similarly, standards-based reporting provides parents, other teachers, and administrators with more useful information, clearly stating expectations and criteria in such a way that a student's "grade" is more than an arbitrary mark. Guskey and Bailey elaborate as follows:

- A standards-based report card or reporting tool must clearly describe what students are expected to know and be able to do.
- A standards-based report card or reporting tool must clearly describe a student's level of knowledge and performance of the standards. (Thomas Guskey and Jane M. Bailey, *Developing Standards-based Report Cards* [Thousand Oaks, CA: Corwin Press, 2010])

According to Dr. Robert Marzano, Thomas Guskey, and others, separate reporting of academic achievement and behavioral indicators more clearly communicates areas of strength and concern to the student, other educators, and parents. Colet Bartow provides an example of a standards-based report in Figure 8.16.

Performance-based Report: 2nd Quarter 2012–2013 Student: Mike Info					
10th Grade	Academic Achievement	Information Literacy	Participation	Citizenship	
Communication Arts	NP	NP	NP	NP	
Social Studies	NP				
Mathematics	P				
Science	P				

Performance Level Key:	Reported Performance Areas:
Novice (N): below the standard Nearing Proficiency (NP): approaching the standard Proficient (P): meets the standard Advanced (A): exceeds the standard **See attached summary of standards for 2nd quarter.**	Academic Achievement: Indicators of student knowledge within a subject area. Information Literacy: Description of student performance in effectively using and producing ideas and information. Participation: Behavioral indicators for the student's interaction and engagement in the classroom. Citizenship: Behavioral indicators for the student's interaction in the school community.

Synthesis: Organize from multiple sources; present the information
Summary of standards

Communication Arts	Writing 5.7 Identify the purpose, audience, and format in one's own writing Writing 5.11 Identify the owner of ideas and information
Science	1 (Rationale): Students must understand the process of science—how information is gathered, evaluated, and communicated to others.
Social Studies	1.1 Identify and practice the steps of an inquiry process (i.e., create a new product, etc.).
Technology	2.3 Communicate the results of research and learning with others using digital tools
Information Literacy	2.6 Create a product that presents findings. 4.2 Identify the owner of ideas and information.

Big6 by the Month: Synthesis (2011). Developed by Colet Bartow.

Figure 8.16 Sample Standards-Based Report

Summary

Based on Big6 as well as ICT literacy and Common Core perspectives, Synthesis includes the most extensive set of skills and understandings in the entire information problem-solving process. No single content area can fully cover what students need to learn about Synthesis in order to be successful in school and beyond. English and Language Arts standards for writing and communication all relate to Synthesis as do ICT Literacy standards on presentation software, graphics, and multi-media products. Other subject areas also emphasize Synthesis, e.g., creating maps, charts, and tables in social studies, lab reports and graphic display in science, creating graphs in math.

The Big6 by the Month program reinforces Synthesis learning from all these content areas, helps the entire school to coordinate Synthesis learning, and fills in gaps not included in other curricular areas. For example, the Big6 by the Month program emphasizes the importance of producing products for a particular audience in an appropriate format.

The Big6 program also stresses creating a "culture of citing" by explaining why and how to give credit and expecting students to cite sources in an established format.

Clear grade level objectives that grow in sophistication and complexity as students progress through the grades are crucial for Synthesis. Lesson plans developed in conjunction with local content assignments emphasize each of the grade level objectives. The results of Synthesis offer direct *evidence* for assessment, making it relatively easy to apply predefined *criteria* by which students will be assessed. We encourage you to give students the opportunity to self-assess and report before they submit their assignments. Finally, we recommend program reporting that includes documenting student achievement in a standards-based format.

Online Resources

Useful Sites: Organizing Information

"PowerPoint for Note-taking Template," by Mike Eisenberg, http://big6.com/media/freestuff/Big6-Blank-Note taking-Template.ppt

"PowerPoint for Note-taking" (YouTube video), by Mike Eisenberg, https://youtu.be/2xnNGHWwkgk

Graphic Organizers, http://www.graphic.org/goindex.html

Evernote, http://evernote.com/

Useful Sites: Rubrics

"Assessment and Rubric Information," by Kathy Schrock, http://www.schrockguide.net/assessment-and-rubrics .html

RubiStar (sample and customizable rubrics), http://rubistar.4teachers.org/

"Empower Students through Self-Assessment," by Violet Harada and Patricia Louis, can be accessed from http://aasl11harada.wikispaces.com/Resources

"Plagiarism-Proofing Assignments," by Doug Johnson, http://www.doug-johnson.com/dougwri/plagiarism -proofing-assignments.html

Jay McTighe and Grant Wiggins, *Understanding by Design*, http://shop.ascd.org/Default.aspx?TabID=55& ProductId=406&Understanding-by-design-expanded-2nd-edition

Useful Site: Tablet and Web 2.0 Applications

Kathy Schrock's "Guide to Everything: Bloomin' Apps," iPad, Google, Android, and Web 2.0 applications to support each of the levels of Bloom's Revised Taxonomy, http://www.schrockguide.net/bloomin-apps.html

Useful Sites: Citing Sources

"Using the Big6 to Prevent Plagiarism," by Ru Story-Huffman, http://big6.com/pages/lessons/articles/using-the -big6-to-prevent-plagiarism.php

"Plagiarism-Proofing Assignments," by Doug Johnson, http://www.doug-johnson.com/dougwri/plagiarism -proofing-assignments.html

"Citing Sources: A Quick and Graphic Guide," by Kate Hart (shows Harry Potter characters "quoting" J. K. Row-ling in various unacceptable ways), http://www.katehart.net/2012/06/citing-sources-quick-and-graphic-guide .html

Selected Interactive Online Citation Generators

Bibme, http://www.bibme.org/

Citation Machine, http://citationmachine.net/

EasyBib: Automatic Bibliography and Citation Maker, http://www.easybib.com/

DocsCite, citation generator for government documents (APA and MLA styles only) from Arizona State University Libraries, www.asu.edu/lib/hayden/govdocs/docscite/docscite.htm

KnightCite, citation generator from the Hekman Library, http://www.calvin.edu/library/knightcite/index.php

Noodletools, http://www.noodletools.com/

Refworks, http://www.refworks.com/

Zotero, A free, easy-to-use Firefox extension to help you collect, manage, and cite your research sources, http://www.zotero.org/

Chapter 9

"HOW HIGH THE SKY?"

April:
Evaluation

6.1 Judge the product.
6.2 Judge the process.

In This Chapter

- ❑ Introduction: Evaluation
- ❑ Defined: Standards and Grade Level Objectives
- ❑ Predictable: Lessons and Assessments
- ❑ Measured: Student Self-Assessment, Performance Descriptors
- ❑ Reported: Standards-Based Reports
- ❑ Summary
- ❑ Online Resources

Introduction: Evaluation

Evaluation is a broad-based process that encompasses a wide range of specific problem-solving actions. For example, "evaluation of information" is part of each Big6 stage:

- **Task Definition:** evaluation of the problem and information requirements.
- **Information Seeking Strategies**: evaluation of sources applying criteria related to relevance and credibility.
- **Location & Access:** evaluation of search terms and commands.
- **Use of Information:** evaluation of value and usefulness of specific information gathered.
- **Synthesis:** evaluation of how to organize and present information.
- **Evaluation:** evaluation of the final product and personal or group information problem-solving abilities.

In previous chapters, we have included explanations and practical examples of "evaluation of information" standards, lessons, and measurement of skills and subskills in the context of specific Big6 stages. Here, we turn to Big6 stage 6, Evaluation itself. The focus here is to make judgments about (1) the final result or product of the information process and (2) individual or group competence and skills in information problem-solving.

6.0 Evaluation

    6.1 Judge the product (effectiveness and quality)

    6.2 Judge the process (personal efficiency)

Evaluating the product (6.1) can be formative or summative. *Formative* evaluation takes place during the process, while students are working on their projects, reports, or papers. Formative evaluation should encourage students to revise or rework a product to improve the final version. For example, while working on an assignment, students can assess whether they are making progress on completing the task as defined. Sometimes students will realize they don't quite understand the task and need to review requirements and adjust, narrow, or expand the task.

Summative evaluation takes place at the conclusion of an assignment. Students should be able to judge whether they successfully solved the information problem or made a good decision. They should be able to determine the quality of their final products in comparison to clearly stated criteria for judging quality.

Examples of Evaluation 6.1 include students being able to do the following:

- Evaluate multimedia presentations for both content and format.
- Determine whether they are on the right track in their science experiment.
- Judge the effectiveness of three different TV commercials.
- Rate their projects based on a predetermined set of criteria.

Depending on your students' projects or information needs, there may be other variations to these questions, such as the following:

- Was the information problem solved?
- Was the need met?
- Was the decision made?
- Was the situation resolved?
- Does the product satisfy the requirements as originally defined?

If a student's answer is "no" (such as when the project or report is incomplete), he or she will need to go back and redefine the task and reinitiate the Big6 Skills process.

In Big6 stage 6.2, students reflect on their personal success in overall information problem-solving as well as their strengths and weaknesses in specific Big6 skills or subskills. We want students to continue to improve their Big6 skills by being able to assess their performance. One useful approach is to have students reflect individually or as a class on which Big6 stages were easy and which ones were hard (and why) or how they could improve next time to be more efficient as well as effective.

Examples of Evaluation 6.2 include students being able to do the following:

- Assess their confidence in answering a question about the structure and function of the human heart.
- Thoughtfully consider how well they were able to use electronic sources throughout their project.
- Talk about what was most difficult in completing an assignment.
- Compare the amount of time spent thinking about an art project and the amount of time actually working on the same art project.
- Reflect on their level of personal effort and time spent during their work on the assignment.

Defined

In April, we want to offer an instructional plan that provides a school-wide focus on **Evaluation**. Evaluation is the critical final stage of the Big6 Skills, which sets it apart from other research models. When students can accurately judge their own product and process, teachers can expect them to improve in subsequent projects. The Big6 by the Month program *defines* each stage of the Big6 in terms of standards augmented by grade level objectives or learning expectations.

Standards for Evaluation

Only two sets of information and communication technology (ICT) literacy standards address evaluation, but they both incorporate Big6 terminology, emphasizing assessment of both *product* and *process* (see Figure 9.1).

ICT Literacy Standards Related to Evaluation	
AASL	3.4.1 Assess the **processes** by which learning was achieved in order to revise strategies and learn more effectively in the future. 3.4.2 Assess the quality and **effectiveness** of the learning **product**.
NETS-S	1a. Apply existing knowledge to generate new ideas, **products**, or **processes**. 2b. Communicate information and ideas **effectively** to multiple audiences using a variety of media and formats. 5b. Exhibit a positive attitude toward using technology that supports collaboration, learning, and productivity.

Compiled by Janet Murray from *AASL Standards for the 21st-Century Learner*, © 2007, American Association of School Librarians, http://www.ala.org/aasl/standards; and ISTE, National Educational Technology Standards (NETS-S) for Students.

Figure 9.1 ICT Literacy Standards Related to Evaluation

As in previous months, teachers and students need to see that information literacy skills are important in all areas of the curriculum, not just as part of research. The Common Core State Standards Initiative provides a national perspective on what high school graduates must know and be able to do in order to succeed in entry-level college courses or the workplace. Some of these standards pertain directly to both substages of Big6 stage 6, Evaluation (see Figure 9.2).

Common Core Standards Related to Evaluation	
Writing	5. Develop and strengthen writing as needed by planning, **revising**, editing, rewriting, or trying a new approach. 10. Write routinely over extended time frames (time for research, **reflection**, and **revision**) and shorter time frames (a single sitting or a day or two) for a range of tasks, purposes, and audiences.
Mathematical Practices	1. Make sense of problems and persevere in solving them: . . . monitor and **evaluate progress**. 8. Look for and express regularity in repeated reasoning: . . . continually **evaluate the reasonableness of** their immediate **results**.

Compiled by Janet Murray and Colet Bartow from The Common Core State Standards Initiative, http://www.corestandards.org/the-standards. See "Big6™ Skills Aligned with Common Core Standards," http://janetsinfo.com/Big6_CCSSIStds.htm.

Figure 9.2 Common Core Standards Related to Evaluation

Two Common Core Standards related to writing emphasize **revision**: reflecting on the adequacy of the product allows students to improve (develop and strengthen) their writing. "Mathematical Practices" standards expect students to evaluate their progress in solving a problem, as well as the reasonableness of their solutions. There are many more Common Core Standards related to Synthesis than to any other Big6 stage, but using thoughtful self-assessment and formative feedback will encourage and enable students to improve their performance on future assignments.

Examine your state's content standards to find similar wording. (Use the *Standards Template* in the "Templates" section in the appendices.)

Grade Level Objectives

For each Big6 or Super3 stage, our goal as teachers, technology teachers, or teacher-librarians is to identify "power" information literacy goals and learning objectives for all students in our school. These goals and objectives should link to relevant national or local learning standards. Figure 9.3 displays Montana's *Essential Learning Expectations for Information Literacy* related to Evaluation. Notice the emphasis on evaluating both *product* and *process*.

Use the *Grade Level Objectives Template* to create learning expectations for each grade level at your school.

Cross-Grade Objective	Grades					
	K	**1**	**2**	**3**	**4**	**5**
3.1 Assess the quality of the product: *criteria*.	A. Compare product to criteria.	A. Compare product to criteria.	A. Compare product to criteria.	A. Compare product to criteria.	A. Compare product to criteria.	A. Identify product's strengths and weaknesses according to task criteria.
3.1 Assess the quality of the product: *reflect*.	B. Reflect on final product.	B. Reflect on final product.	B. Judge the final product.	B. Judge the final product.	B. Judge the final product.	B. Critique final product.
3.1 Assess the quality of the product: *improve*.	C. Explore ideas for improvement of the product.	C. Discuss ideas for improvement of the product.	C. Generate ideas for improvement of the product.	C. Generate ideas for improvement of the product.	C. Generate ideas for improvement of the product.	C. Identify areas for improvement of the product.
3.2 BM 8 Evaluate how the *process* met the need for information.	B. Discuss how well the process worked.	B. Discuss how well the process worked.	B. Describe how well the process worked.	B. Describe how well the process worked.	C. Describe how well the process worked.	B. Describe how well the process worked. D. Discuss areas for improvement in the process.

Cross-Grade Objective	Grades				
	6	7	8	9–10	11–12
3.1 BM 8 Assess the quality and effectiveness of the product: *criteria*.	A. Describe product's strengths and weaknesses according to task criteria.	A. Evaluate product's strengths and weaknesses according to task criteria.	A. Self-evaluate product's strengths and weaknesses according to task criteria.	A. Use guidelines to self-assess the product.	A. Self-assess the product.
3.1 BM 8 Assess the quality and effectiveness of the product: *critique*.	B. Critique final product.	B. Critique final product.	B. Use guidelines to compare self-evaluation to teacher and peer evaluations.	B. Use guidelines to compare self-evaluation to teacher and peer evaluations.	B. Compare self-assessment to teacher and peer evaluations.
3.1 BM 8 Assess the quality and effectiveness of the product: *improve*.	C. Identify areas for improvement of the product.	C. Identify areas for improvement of the product.	C. Identify areas for improvement of the product.	C. Revise, edit, rewrite based on assessments.	C. Revise, edit, rewrite based on assessments.
3.2 BM 8 Evaluate how the *process* met the need for information.	A. Examine task-completion process. B. Identify areas for improvement in the process.	A. Examine task-completion process. B. Identify areas for improvement in the process.	A. Appraise task-completion process. B. Identify areas for improvement in the process.	A. Examine the strengths and weaknesses of the process. C. Reflect on the process to make improvements.	A. Judge the strengths and weaknesses of the process. C. Reflect on the process to make improvements.

Compiled by Janet Murray from Montana's *Essential Learning Expectations for Information Literacy,* http://www.opi.mt.gov/pdf/Standards/10FebELE_LibMedia.xls.

BM = benchmark

Figure 9.3 Grade Level Objectives Related to Evaluation

Predictable

The Big6 by the Month program is *predictable* because each month is devoted to a particular stage of the Big6 Skills. If you are responsible for information literacy instruction, you need to develop a plan related to the school's calendar, organization, and schedule. Strive to identify one or two major assignments for each grade and teacher, then develop Evaluation lessons targeted to classroom assignments or units.

Lesson Ideas for Evaluation

6.0 Evaluation

6.1 Judge the product (effectiveness and quality)

6.2 Judge the process (personal efficiency)

In the Big6 process, students engaged in Evaluation judge their results (in relation to the assignment) as well as their performance in the Big6 process or any specific stage. Judging the product (6.1) can be either formative, which enables students to revise before submitting a final product, or summative, the final product. Judging the process (6.2) is future looking, helping students to learn and improve.

One clear way to make instruction and learning about Evaluation more predictable—in terms of product or process—is to focus on rubrics (also called scoring guides). A good rubric should identify the evidence for evaluation as well as the criteria applied to that evidence. Teachers can provide the assessment rubric to students, or it is often effective to engage students in creating the rubric or revising a draft rubric.

Timing is also important to maximize the meaningful use of rubrics. For example, sharing a rubric at the same time the assignment is given will immediately help the students to better define the task and know what is expected of them. Sharing a rubric for an assignment with the students also facilitates self-assessment *before* students submit a final assignment. The rubric gives them the opportunity to reflect and revise according to the learning criteria defined by the standards. (See also Chapter 8.) Standards and expectations often refer to self-evaluation; notice the category "compare self-evaluation to teacher and peer evaluations" in the grade level objectives above.

Figures 9.4 through 9.7 are examples of self-assessment instruments and rubrics for the Super3 and Big6 for students at various grade levels, from early elementary to high school.

Super3
- Plan
- Do
- Review

Name:______________________________

Review 2

I followed all directions. 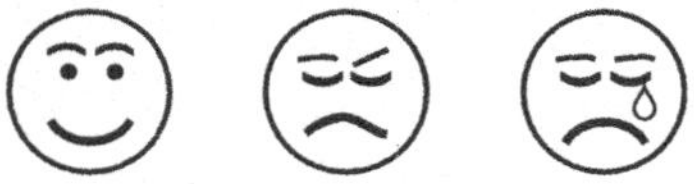

I found all the information I needed. 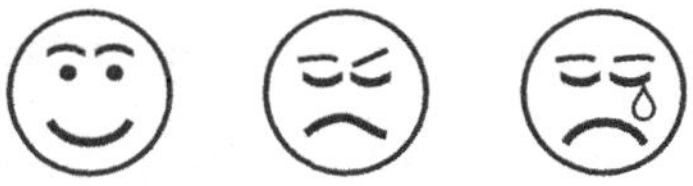

I answered all questions. 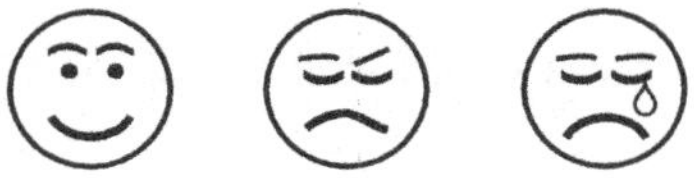

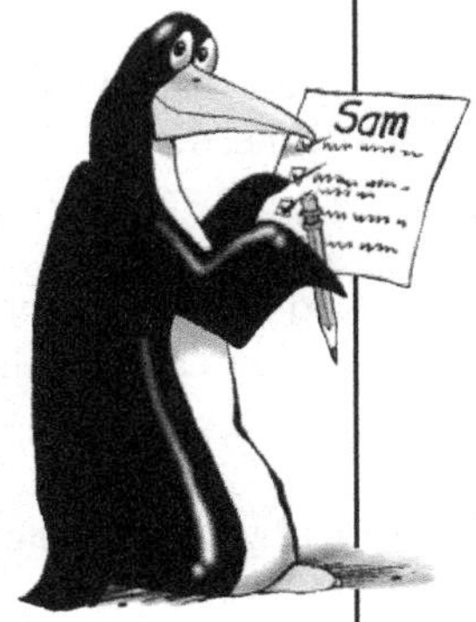

I did my best work. 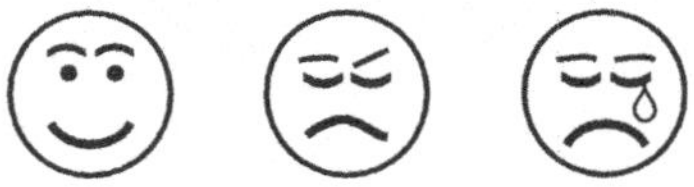

I checked my work for mistakes. 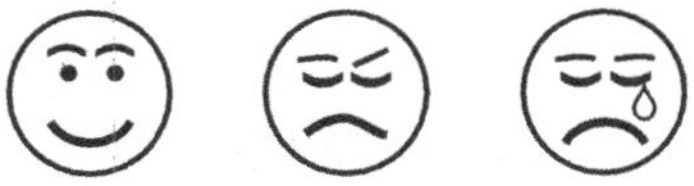

Figure 4.37 **Review 2**

80 *The Super3™: Information Skills for Young Learners*

Figure 9.4 Sample Super3™ Self-Assessment Review

Check List For Completing a Science Fair Project

Before you take your project to school or to the science fair, answer the following questions to make sure that you have done your best work:

1. Evaluate your method.

Was the method the best way to prove or disprove the hypothesis?
___ yes ___ no

If you answered "no," then what would you change about the method? Add this to your conclusion.

2. Evaluate your background research.

Did your background research give you adequate information about your subject to help you start planning your experiment? ___ yes ___ no

If not, what information should you have researched?

Is it too late to add this information to your report? ___ yes ___ no

3. Evaluate your display.

Does your display contain your name and a title?
___ yes ___ no

Is the displayed text word processed, neat and organized using headings and subheadings?
___ yes ___ no

Do the text, graphics, and photographs help the judges and audience understand your process and results?
___ yes ___ no

Are your materials dangerous?
___ yes ___ no

Can your materials break or spill and harm young children who may look at your project?
___ yes ___ no

If you answered "yes," what can you do to prevent an injury? This is very important!

Would you be proud for anyone to view this project?
___ yes ___ no

From the Big6™ Science Fair Organizer by Barbara A. Jansen, available http://www.big6.com/kids.

Barbara Jansen, http://big6.com/media/freestuff/checklist_science_fair.pdf

Figure 9.5 Checklist for Completing a Science Fair Project

CATEGORY	Exemplary	Proficient	Partially Proficient	Incomplete	POINTS
Research Questions	*3 points*	*2 points*	*1 point*	*0 points*	___ / 3
	Wrote thoughtful, creative, well-worded specific questions that were relevant to the assigned topic.	Wrote well-worded, specific questions that were relevant to the assigned topic.	Wrote questions which lacked focus, were poorly stated, and were not entirely relevant to the assigned topic.	Wrote questions which lacked a specific focus, were poorly stated, and not relevant to the assigned topic.	
Selection of Sources	*3 points*	*2 points*	*1 point*	*0 points*	___ / 3
	Identified highly appropriate sources in a variety of formats (books, journals, electronic sources).	Identified mostly appropriate sources in a variety of formats (books, journals, electronic sources).	Identified a few appropriate sources but made little attempt to balance format types.	Identified no appropriate sources in any format.	
Note-taking & Keywords	*3 points*	*2 points*	*1 point*	*0 points*	___ / 3
	Extracted relevant information.	Extracted mostly relevant information.	Extracted a lot of information which wasn't relevant.	Extracted irrelevant information.	
	Brainstormed keywords, categories, related terms that were effective in researching the questions.	Selected mostly effective keywords to use in researching the questions.	Selected some keywords that were not effective in researching the questions.	Selected no effective keywords to use in researching the questions.	
	Wrote notes including succinct key facts which directly answered all of the research questions and were written in the student's own words.	Wrote notes which included facts that answered most of the research questions and were written in the student's own words.	Wrote notes which included irrelevant facts which did not answer the research questions. Some notes were copied directly from the original source.	Wrote notes which included a majority of facts which did not answer the research questions. Most or all notes were copied word-for-word from the original source.	

http://www2.uwstout.edu/content/profdev/rubrics/middlelschresearchrubric.html

Figure 9.6 Sample Research Process Rubric: Middle School

Student Self Evaluation Sheet

NAME: DATE:

PROJECT:

✓   What did you enjoy most about this project? Why?

✓   What part of this project did you do the best on? Why?

✓   Which part of this project was most difficult for you to do well on? Why?

✓   What one concept did you find most interesting to learn about? What did you learn about that concept?

✓   If you had to do another project like this, what could you do to get a better result?

Adapted from Bob Berkowitz, "Civil War: A Study in Change," http://big6.com/pages/lessons/lessons/u.s.-history-civil-war-a-study-in-change.php

Figure 9.7 Student Self-Evaluation Checklist: Secondary Level

Following are two examples of using these types of evaluation tools with assignments and units. The first (Figure 9.8) involves an extensive middle school science fair project; the second (Figure 9.9) is a culminating self-assessment for a social studies project.

Big6™ Stage:	Evaluation
Grade Level:	5–8
GL Objective:	To engage in scientific investigation
Subject Area:	Science
Unit Focus:	Science fair project

Figure 9.8 Middle School Level Evaluation Lesson in Context

Subject Area Lesson Goal: Student(s) will propose a question or hypothesis, engage in background research, develop an experimental apparatus or procedure that will produce data, analyze data, and draw conclusions to prove (or disprove) the hypothesis.

Learning Activity:

1. Remind the students of the assignment.
2. Discuss the Big6 process.
3. Introduce formative assessment using the assignment guidelines, a checklist, and a rubric (see Figures 9.5 and 9.6).
4. Have each student complete the checklist and rubric.
5. Discuss levels of performance and how to revise and resubmit.

Assessment:

- Evidence: Checklist and rubric.
- Criteria: Quality of product, completeness, performance levels.

Big6™ Stage:	Evaluation
Grade Level:	10
GL Objective:	Perspectives of key historical figures
Subject Area:	Social Studies
Unit Focus:	Research project

Figure 9.9 Grade 10 Evaluation Lesson in Context

Subject Area Lesson Goal: Each student will research and present on the social, political, or economic perspective of one key historical figure.

Learning Activity:

1. Students complete the self-evaluation checklist (Figure 9.7).
2. In their groups, students discuss the most difficult parts of the assignment and how they might improve in the future.
3. The entire class discusses the project in terms of what they might do differently in the future.

Assessment:

- Evidence: Self-evaluation checklist.
- Criteria: Complete, insightful, logical.

Measured

It is important to consider assessment strategies *before* giving assignments to students. This approach is sometimes called "backward design" and is detailed in Jay McTighe and Grant Wiggins's *Understanding by Design* (http://shop.ascd.org/Default.aspx?TabID=55&ProductId=406&Understanding-by-design-expanded-2nd-edition). A unit plan based on the backward design model contains the elements shown in Figure 9.10.

Unit Plan		
Desired Results	Big6 Stage 6, Evaluation	Content Standards
	Enduring Understandings	Essential Questions
Assessment Evidence	Performance Tasks	Content Assessment
	Information Skills Assessment/ Performance Rubric	Content Evidence (Product)
Learning Plan	Lesson Progression	Materials and Resources
	Websites/Reference	Other Details

Big6 by the Month: Evaluation (2013). Designed by Colet Bartow.

Figure 9.10 Sample Unit Plan, Evaluation

"Enduring Understandings" and "Essential Questions" should include content-specific knowledge and skills, as well as information skills. Evaluation is part of each and every stage of the process, but in the month of April we are really focused on evaluation of the quality of work and how well students use the problem-solving process to complete projects and assignments.

Rubrics

We introduced the concept of rubrics above and expand it further here with additional examples. Students need to know whether or not they have achieved the desired information literacy goals and objectives. This type of evaluation requires unambiguous criteria that are easily applied to the evidence. When developing rubrics and criteria, we recommend asking the following questions:

- Are the learning criteria clear?
- Are the learning criteria measureable?
- Are the learning criteria stated in student-friendly language?
- Are the learning criteria focused on the learning objective?
- Are the learning criteria reflected in the evidence?

Figure 9.11 provides detailed criteria applied to evidence for a typical fifth-grade "States" report. Notice how the criteria are linked to specific evidence within the report. Figure 9.12 takes the sample rubric and turns it into a self-assessment instrument for students.

5th-Grade State Report	Standards: Information Literacy: A student must evaluate the product and learning process. Social Studies: Students apply geographic knowledge and skills (e.g., location, place, human/environment interactions, movement, and regions). Writing: Students will write to communicate effectively for a variety of purposes and audiences. Visual Arts: Students develop and refine arts skills and techniques to express ideas, pose and solve problems, and discover meaning.		
Evidence	*Evaluation Criteria*	*Due Date*	*Complete*
Written Reports • Cover • Cover sheet • 3 Paragraph Expository Report • Cited Sources • Report Checklist 6+1 Traits Rubric http://education northwest.org/traits/traits-rubrics	Ideas Organization Voice Word Choice Sentence Fluency Conventions Completeness Accuracy		
Maps • Land forms • Political • Products, Economy or Weather Creating Map Rubric http://rubi star.4teachers.org/index.php ?screen=ShowRubric&rubric_id =1954702&	Neatness Completeness Accuracy		
State Brochure • State seal • State flag • State bird • State tree • State flower • License plate • Timeline of state history • Brochure Checklist 6+1 Traits Rubric http://education northwest.org/traits/traits-rubrics	Ideas Organization Voice Word Choice Sentence Fluency Conventions Completeness Presentation		
Multi-media • State song • Tourism Video • Video Production Checklist	Creativity Organization Presentation		
Other • State recipe • Taste Test Rubric	Authenticity Taste Presentation		

Compiled by Colet Bartow. Big6 by the Month: Evaluation (2012).

Figure 9.11 Sample Rubric: Fifth-Grade State Report

5th-Grade State Report Evidence	Evaluation Criteria	Self-Evaluation Statements	Yes	Not Yet
Written Reports • Cover • Cover sheet • 3 Paragraph Expository Report • Cited Sources • Report Checklist 6+1 Traits Rubric	Ideas	I have included ideas that I knew before about my state. I have included ideas that were new and surprising to me about my state. My ideas really give accurate and specific details to describe my state. The details are focused on my state and don't wander into other states or topics.		
If you answered "not yet" for your self-evaluation, please explain what you feel you need to do to get to "yes."				

Compiled by Colet Bartow. Big6 by the Month: Evaluation (2012).

Figure 9.12 Sample Self-Assessment Instrument

With evidence and criteria identified and defined, the last step in effective use of rubrics is to determine and state the specific descriptor levels of proficiency for each criterion. Figures 9.13 and 9.14 provide examples of proficiency levels for evaluating both the product and process at three grade levels: 2, 8, and 12.

Grade 2: Standard 3—A student must evaluate the product and learning process.		Grade 8: Standard 3—A student must evaluate the product and learning process.		Grade 12: Standard 3—A student must evaluate the product and learning process.	
Criteria	Proficient	Criteria	Proficient	Criteria	Proficient
1. Assess the quality of the product.	A. Compare product to criteria. B. Judge final product. C. Generate ideas for improvement of the product.	1. Assess the quality and effectiveness of the product.	A. Self-evaluate product's strengths and weaknesses according to task criteria. B. Use guidelines to compare self-evaluation to teacher and peer evaluations. C. Identify areas for improving the product.	1. Assess the quality and effectiveness of the product.	A. Self-assess the product according to task criteria. B. Compare self-assessment to teacher and peer evaluations. C. Consider revision, editing, rewriting based on assessments.

Compiled by Colet Bartow. Big6 by the Month: Evaluation (2012).

Figure 9.13 Sample Criteria and Proficiency for Evaluation 6.1

Grade 2: Standard 3—A student must evaluate the product and learning process.		Grade 8: Standard 3—A student must evaluate the product and learning process.		Grade 12: Standard 3—A student must evaluate the product and learning process.	
Criteria	Proficient	Criteria	Proficient	Criteria	Proficient
2. Describe the process.	A. Explain the steps that were used in own words. B. Describe how well the process worked.	2. Evaluate how the process met the need for information.	A. Appraise task completion process. B. Identify areas for improvement in the process.	2. Evaluate the process in order to revise strategies.	A. Judge the strengths and weaknesses of the process. B. Evaluate time management throughout the process. C. Reflect on the process to make improvements.

Compiled by Colet Bartow. Big6 by the Month: Evaluation (2012).

Figure 9.14 Sample Criteria and Proficiency for Evaluation 6.2

Besides differentiating across grade levels, rubrics also allow a teacher or student to determine and define the levels of performance for each criterion. We refer to these as performance descriptor levels. Figure 9.15 provides a ninth-grade example of performance descriptor levels for Evaluation, that is, judging the product and process, Big6 6.1 and 6.2.

Evaluating the process and product cannot be solely self-guided. Colet Bartow suggests meeting with students individually or in small groups, along with using checklists or rubrics. Students can also self-assess and debrief with other students or in student-led conferences with parents or other significant adults.

9th-Grade Criteria (Benchmark)	Novice	Nearing Proficiency	Proficient	Advanced
1. Assess the quality and effectiveness of the product.	A. Unlikely to self-assess the product accurately. B. Be unlikely to compare self-assessment to teacher and peer evaluations. C. Be unlikely to revise, edit, rewrite.	A. Be likely to use guidelines to realistically self-assess the product. B. Compare self-assessment to teacher and peer evaluations with guidance. C. Be likely to revise, edit, or rewrite based on assessments.	A. Use guidelines to self-assess the product. B. Use guidelines to compare self-assessment to teacher and peer evaluations. C. Revise, edit, rewrite based on assessments.	A. Accurately self-assess the product. B. Engage in a detailed comparison between self-assessment and teacher and peer evaluations. C. Independently revise, edit, rewrite based on peer, teacher, and self-assessment.
2. Evaluate the process in order to revise strategies.	A. Be unlikely to examine the strengths and weaknesses of the process. B. Be unlikely to evaluate time management throughout the process. C. Struggle to reflect on the process to make improvements.	A. Be likely to examine the strengths and weaknesses of the process. B. Be likely to evaluate time management at some point during the process. C. Inconsistently reflect on the process to make improvements.	A. Examine the strengths and weaknesses of the process. B. Evaluate time management throughout the process. C. Reflect on the process to make improvements.	A. Critically examine the strengths and weaknesses of the process. B. Consistently evaluate and refine time management throughout the process. C. Consistently reflect on the process to make improvements.

Compiled by Colet Bartow. Big6 by the Month: Evaluation (2013).

Figure 9.15 Sample Performance Descriptors for Evaluation (Grade 9)

Our final example, Figure 9.16, is a self-assessment that incorporates all the preceding Big6 stages in an instrument focused on the *process*.

While we have focused here on measurement of student learning, we also encourage assessing instructor performance: How well is the instructor able to design and deliver Big6 or Super3 instruction that is integrated with subject area curriculum? For example, Barbara Jansen suggests evaluating the teacher's delivery of Big6 units with the following questions:

- How successful was this Big6 unit? Will you teach it again?
- How successful was the level of student engagement?
- How effectively were the learning objectives or standards met?
- What do you need to consider or change the next time you teach this unit? (Barbara Jansen, "Evaluating Big6 Units," http://big6.com/media/freestuff/Evaluating_Big6_Units.pdf)

Big6™ Skill	Yes (2)	Almost (1)	No (0)
1. Task Definition 1.1 I defined the information problem. 1.2 I identified the information needed.			
2. Information Seeking Strategies 2.1 I determined all possible sources. 2.2 I selected the best sources.			
3. Location & Access 3.1 I located sources. 3.2 I found information within sources.			
4. Use of Information 4.1 I engaged the information (e.g., read, hear, view, touch). 4.2 I extracted relevant information.			
5. Synthesis 5.1 I organized from multiple sources. 5.2 I presented the information.			
I need to work on:			
I really like:			

Compiled by Colet Bartow. Big6 by the Month: Evaluation (2012).

Figure 9.16 Sample Self-Assessment Instrument (Big6™ Stages)

Reported

We sometimes underestimate the importance of reporting on the means as well as end results of assessment. That's why we encourage Big6 educators to focus on a particular audience (students, parents, administrators, or other teachers) and select from the evidence that students have generated to report how well they have met criteria and how well they have employed the problem-solving process.

It is important to have an organizational structure, expectations, and a container to manage the evidence of learning. How do you currently manage the evidence of student learning that you collect?

We can provide specific beneficial information to parents and caregivers to help them help their students succeed. Sometimes a list of questions can help lead to more productive conversations about what students are expected to know and be able to do. Use parent- and student-friendly language and take time to visit with students and parents about what these stages mean. The important thing is to encourage conversation between parents and students. These conversations serve to reinforce the skills of self-evaluation and allow students to share their learning with confidence.

Sample Message for April:	9th-grade students will be able to:	Questions to ask:
Dear Parents/Guardians: During the month of April, your student will work on a variety of projects and assignments. As part of each project, we will focus on stage 6 of the Big6 information problem-solving model: Evaluation. You can help reinforce these skills by asking your student questions that relate to:	Describe the quality of their project or assignment using the requirements.	Did you complete all of the project or assignment requirements? Did you do your best job on each of the components?
6.1 Judging their work. 6.2 Judging the process of creating projects and assignments. The chart in this message details the skills students will practice and some questions you can ask to help students be successful as they complete assignments and projects. Please contact me if you have any questions. Sincerely, [provide contact information]	Describe the process used to complete the project or assignment. Describe the strengths and weaknesses of their approach to completing the project.	What did you do to manage and organize each of the components of the project or assignment? What would you do differently the next time you have a project or assignment like this?

Big6 by the Month: Evaluation (2013). Developed by Colet Bartow.

Figure 9.17 Sample Report to Parents, Evaluation

Summary

The Big6 by the Month program emphasizes Evaluation skills in the month of April. You can target ICT literacy and Common Core standards by creating grade level objectives to evaluate both the product and the process. Create lesson plans in conjunction with local content assignments to emphasize each of the grade level objectives. Make evaluation *predictable* by distributing rubrics with the assignment. Clearly identify the *evidence* and *criteria* by which students will be assessed. Give students the opportunity to self-assess before they submit their assignments. Consider a variety of methods to manage the evidence of student learning.

Online Resources

Useful Sites: Self-Assessment

Bob Berkowitz, "Civil War: A Study in Change," http://big6.com/pages/lessons/lessons/u.s.-history-civil-war-a-study-in-change.php

"Evaluation: The Final Step," by Ru Story-Huffman, http://big6.com/pages/lessons/lessons/evaluation-the-final-step.php

"Rubric for Assessment: Integrated Problem Solving Model," http://big6.com/pages/lessons/assignments/rubric-for-assessment-integrated-problem-solving-model.php

"Big6 in Action: Evaluation" (checklists), http://big6.com/pages/kids/grades-k-6/articles-k-6/big6-in-action-evaluation.php?searchresult=1&sstring=evaluation#wb_122

"Have Students Use the Big6 to Solve Problems," by Melissa Thibault (includes tips to encourage self-reflection), http://instructify.com/2010/02/24/big6-problemsolving/

"Empower Students through Self-Assessment," by Violet Harada and Patricia Louis, can be accessed from http://aasl11harada.wikispaces.com/Resources

TRAILS: Tools for Real-Time Assessment of Information Literacy Skills, http://www.trails-9.org/

Useful Sites: Rubrics

"Assessment and Rubric Information," by Kathy Schrock, http://www.schrockguide.net/assessment-and-rubrics.html

"Rubrics and Evaluation Resources," *MidLink Magazine*, http://ncsu.edu/midlink/ho.html

RubiStar (sample and customizable rubrics), http://rubistar.4teachers.org/

Jay McTighe and Grant Wiggins, *Understanding by Design* (http://shop.ascd.org/Default.aspx?TabID=55&ProductId=406&Understanding-by-design-expanded-2nd-edition)

Useful Site: Evaluating Instruction

"Evaluating Big6 Units," by Barbara Jansen, http://big6.com/media/freestuff/Evaluating_Big6_Units.pdf

Chapter 10

"AND IN THE END"

May:
Culminating Activities

In This Chapter

❏ Introduction: Bringing It All Together

❏ Defined: Standards, Assignment Organizers

❏ Predictable: Examples from Washington State OSPI

❏ Measured: Rubrics, Self-Assessment, Sample Unit Plan, Portfolio Evidence, Evaluating Instruction

❏ Reported: TRAILS Reports; Report to Parents; Checklists for Teachers, Teacher-librarians, and Instructional Leaders

❏ Summary

❏ Online Resources

Introduction: Bringing It All Together

In May, we are nearing the end of the Big6 by the Month journey, as we engage in culminating activities that reinforce skills and knowledge gained throughout the school year. But while we are concluding instruction for this year, we are certainly not doing so for the program as a whole. In fact, one of the most powerful aspects of the Big6 by the Month program is the continuity of learning from year to year. The Super3/Big6 curriculum spirals upward in complexity and sophistication of skills taught and learned. Students are continually reminded of skills and knowledge gained in previous years and how they will build on those skills in future years.

A "culminating project" can be an effective curriculum strategy to tie together the various skills, techniques, tools, approaches, and understandings learned throughout the school year. The culminating project offers the opportunity to review, reinforce, emphasize, and assess the ICT skills learned throughout the year as well as students' knowledge and use of the overall Big6 information problem-solving process.

Figure 10.1 is a framework for planning a culminating project that covers all four elements of the Big6 by the Month program. For example, for *Defined* we determine important power objectives related to standards that focus on the overall process and integration of skills. For *Predictable* we recommend including a lesson on the full Super3 or Big6 process and Task Definition as well as other lessons as determined desirable or necessary. *Measured* includes using a Super3 or Big6 planner to establish and reinforce checkpoints at key stages of the process and also as evidence

---

Defined	Predictable	Measured	Reported
The full Super3 or Big6 process and the project.	Initial lesson on the project goals and the full Super3 or Big6 process.	Establish checkpoints for key stages or all six stages.	After initial lesson, report to classroom or other involved teachers on student readiness.
Use some form of Super3/Big6 planner.	Task Definition lesson.	Use Big6 planner as evidence for planning and at checkpoints. Establish criteria.	Provide feedback to students (and teachers) at checkpoints.
Determine power grade level objectives to emphasize.	Other lessons as needed (determined by classroom teacher, teacher-librarian, tech teacher, etc.).	Determine Big6 objectives to assess. Identify evidence (beyond planner). Establish criteria.	Final assessment and report to students and parents.

Figure 10.1 Big6™ by the Month Plan for a Culminating Project

of performance. The *Reported* element includes reporting *during* the project to involve teachers in student readiness as well as performance at the different checkpoints.

Of course, a culminating project is not required for a complete and effective Big6 by the Month program. Any final assignment or assessment (including end-of-the-year exams) can serve as the foundation for a full review, reinforcement, and check of the Super3 or Big6 process.

Defined

As discussed, we recommend planning a culminating activity near the end of the academic year to reinforce and evaluate the Big6 Skills learning over the course of the Big6 by the Month program.

The advantages of culminating activities include providing the following:

- An opportunity for students to demonstrate the Super3 or Big6 and ICT literacy skills they have learned.
- An opportunity for students to demonstrate improvement over their March Synthesis project using the Evaluation skills they learned in April.
- Opportunities for teachers and instructional leaders to assess the impact of the Big6 by the Month program.

The Big6 by the Month program *defines* each stage of the Big6 in terms of *standards* augmented by *grade level objectives* or *learning expectations*.

Standards for Culminating Activities

The culmination of a year studying the Super3 and Big6 Skills should ask students to create a final product that requires them to answer an essential question by evaluating, collecting, and synthesizing information. Information and communication technology (ICT) literacy standards describe the goals of this final project (see Figure 10.2).

The Common Core provides another set of standards—particularly those that relate directly to creating a final product. Mastering the Big6 Skills gives students an overall strategy as well as specific skills and techniques necessary to meet the Common Core Standards (see Figure 10.3).

ICT Literacy Standards Related to Culminating Activities	
AASL	1.1.4 **Find**, **evaluate**, and **select** appropriate sources to answer questions. 2.1.1 Apply critical-thinking skills (**analysis, synthesis, evaluation, organization**) to information and knowledge. 3.1.4 Use technology and other information tools to **organize** and **display** knowledge and understanding in ways that others can view, use, and assess.
ACRL	4.3 Communicates the **product** or performance effectively to others.
NETS-S	3b. Locate, organize, analyze, evaluate, synthesize, and ethically use information from a variety of sources and media. 3c. **Evaluate** and **select** information sources and digital tools based on the appropriateness to specific tasks. 2b. **Communicate** information and ideas effectively to multiple audiences using a variety of media and formats.

Compiled by Janet Murray from *AASL Standards for the 21st-Century Learner*, © 2007, American Association of School Librarians, http://www.ala.org/aasl/standards; "Information Literacy Competency Standards for Higher Education," © 2000, Association of College and Research Libraries, http://www.ala.org/ala/mgrps/divs/acrl/standards/informationliteracycompetency.cfm; and ISTE, National Educational Technology Standards (NETS-S) for Students.

Figure 10.2 ICT Literacy Standards Related to Culminating Activities

Common Core Standards Related to Culminating Activities	
Reading	7. **Integrate** and evaluate content presented in diverse media and formats, including visually and quantitatively, as well as in words.
Reading: Informational Text	7. **Integrate** information presented in different media or formats (e.g., visually, quantitatively), as well as in words to develop a coherent understanding of a topic or issue.
Reading: History and Social Studies	7. **Integrate** visual information (e.g., in charts, graphs, photographs, videos, or maps) with other information in print and digital texts.
Writing	2. Write informative/explanatory texts to examine and convey complex ideas and information clearly and accurately through the **effective selection**, **organization**, and **analysis** of content. 4. **Produce** clear and coherent writing in which the development, organization, and style are appropriate to **task, purpose**, and **audience**. 6. Use technology, including the Internet, to **produce** and **publish** writing and to interact and collaborate with others. 8. **Gather relevant information** from multiple print and digital sources, assess the **credibility** and **accuracy** of each source, and **integrate** the information while avoiding plagiarism.
Speaking and Listening	4. **Present** information, findings, and supporting **evidence** such that listeners can follow the line of **reasoning** and the organization, development, and style are appropriate to **task**, **purpose**, and **audience**.
Mathematical Practices	3. Construct viable arguments: . . . justify conclusions. 6. Attend to precision: . . . **communicate** precisely to others.

Compiled by Janet Murray and Colet Bartow from The Common Core State Standards Initiative, http://www.corestandards.org/the-standards. See "Big6™ Skills Aligned with Common Core Standards," http://janetsinfo.com/Big6_CCSSIStds.htm.

Figure 10.3 Common Core Standards Related to Culminating Activities

Assignment Organizer

Assignment: _____   **Due Date:** _____

Complete Big6 Skills #1-5 BEFORE you BEGIN your assignment.

Complete Big6 Skill #6 BEFORE you TURN IN your assignment.

Big6 Skill #1: Task Definition

What does this assignment require me to do?

What information do I need in order to do this assignment?

Big6 Skill #2: Information Seeking Strategies

What sources can I use to do the assignment? Make a list, then circle the best sources.

Big6 Skill #3: Location & Access

Where can I find my sources? Do I need help? If so, who can help me?

Big6 Skill #4: Use of Information

What do I need to do with the information?

_____ read / view / listen

_____ take notes

_____ answer questions

_____ other: _____

_____ chart and/or write an essay

_____ copy and highlight

_____ properly cite

Big6 Skill #5: Synthesis

What product does this assignment require?

Big6 Skill #6: Evaluation

Student self-evaluation checklist:

_____ I did what I was supposed to do (See Big6 #1, Task Definition)

_____ The assignment is complete.

The Big6 Eisenberg & Berkowitz, 1987. Assignment Organizer © Berkowitz & Hopsicker, 1997
Based on The Big6 Workshop Handbook, Implementation and Impact, Fourth Edition, Assignment Organizer, p. 286.

Figure 10.4 Sample of a Big6™ Assignment Organizer

Set checkpoints or milestones to guide students through the entire culminating assignment process. We recommend using some form of Big6 planner or assignment organizer to lay out the checkpoints. This approach encourages students to engage in *formative assessment* so that they can improve their work before turning it in. An example of a Big6 assignment organizer (Figure 10.4) comes from the most recent edition of *The Big6 Workshop Handbook* (2012). It is also available as a template (see the appendices or download an online version from https://sites.google.com/site /big6xthemonth/file-cabinet) for use with your students.

As emphasized, the culminating project is an excellent opportunity to assess, reinforce, and expand on the lessons taught and learned during the course of the year through the Big6 by the Month program.

Barbara Jansen, Big6 educator, has also created assignment organizers based on the Big6 Skills for all levels of students. See the "Online Resources" section at the end of this chapter.

Predictable

For identified grade level Big6 power objectives, connect to subject areas and assignments:

1. Select grade level Big6 power objectives derived from the standards.
2. Identify one to two subject area assignments, by grade and teacher.
3. Develop culminating activities lessons targeted to the assignments.

Make the culminating project *predictable* by distributing the rubric that will be used to evaluate the project at the same time as the assignment. The rubric should reflect the specific goals and learning objectives of the assignment and should be written in language that is easy for students and parents to understand.

There are many forms of culminating projects. Washington State, for example, requires completion of a culminating project to earn a high school diploma. Washington's Office of the Superintendent of Public Instruction (OSPI) recommends districts use the OSPI-Developed Assessments in Social Studies, the Arts, Health and Fitness, and Educational Technology (http://www.k12.wa.us/assessment/OSPI-DevelopedAssessments.aspx).

As stated on the OSPI website, the purpose of the project is to meet statewide goals to:

- encourage students to think analytically, logically, and creatively and to integrate experience and knowledge to solve problems;
- give students a chance to explore a topic in which they have a great interest; and
- offer students an opportunity to apply their learning in a "real world" way.

"As part of the Culminating Project, each student will demonstrate essential skills through reading, writing, speaking, production and/or performance. To complete the project, students may be asked to write a research paper, work with a mentor in school or in the community, present to a community or peer panel, pull together a portfolio of work and/or develop a multimedia presentation" (OSPI, Graduation Requirements, 2013, http://www.k12.wa.us/gradu ationrequirements/Requirement-CulminatingProject.aspx). This page includes links to sample culminating projects (http://www.k12.wa.us/GraduationRequirements/CulminatingProjects/default.aspx).

Many other states and districts have similar requirements or recommendations for culminating projects for high school graduation. And while the goals listed above are highly valuable for high school students, they are also relevant to students at every grade level. There are also benefits beyond the goals stated above, such as the following:

- Reviewing the overall Big6/Super3 information problem-solving process.

- Recognizing how the Big6/Super3 process is widely applicable.

- Facilitating, reviewing, and reinforcing specific Big6 or Super3 skills.

- Encouraging metacognition, that is, an awareness of one's learning style or process.

- Assessing strengths and areas for improvement before students move to the next grade level.

We recommend some form of culminating project or activity for every grade level as part of the Big6 by the Month program.

Lesson Ideas

We highly recommend offering two introductory Big6 lessons to help students begin their culminating project and plan their approach and actions:

1. Task Definition: Review the assignment with the students to emphasize Big6 1.1—the essential requirements (both content and format), and keys to success (including assessment criteria)—and Big6 1.2, the nature, amounts, and types of information needed to fully complete the assignment.

2. Big6 process: Talk through the culminating assignment in terms of each stage of the Big6 process in relation to the requirements of the assignment and valuable actions to help students succeed effectively and efficiently.

The content of the Task Definition lesson is straightforward: focus on the overall goals and requirements of the assignment, topic selection, the various elements that will go into a high-quality product, the nature of the final product, and how the assignment will be assessed. Alternatives for delivering the lesson include small group exercises (e.g., to analyze, identify, and discuss the components of the assignment), followed by debriefing and summarizing; brainstorming tools (e.g., *Kidspiration*) or other types of graphic organizers or worksheets; and presenting tips and techniques in a full class setting.

The goal of the Big6 process lesson is to remind students of the overall information problem-solving process and the various Big6 skills and techniques that they've learned throughout the year, and to emphasize that each student has his or her own unique way of accomplishing each of the Big6 stages—and that's okay! Some form of assignment organizer (see Figure 10.4) is highly useful as a guide for this lesson as well as the overall Big6 approach to the culminating assignment.

Other lessons can be offered based on identified student need or request. In most schools, individuals or groups of students will have time to work on their assignments during the school day. Big6 instruction is likely to be more decentralized: one-on-one or small group. We recommend offering short mini-lessons to the entire class only when it is clear that many students are raising similar questions or are having the same difficulties. Big6 topics that may benefit from special mini-lessons include the following:

- **Task Definition**
  - Topic selection
  - Asking good questions
  - Using primary vs. secondary information sources
- **Information Seeking Strategies**
  - Identifying unique sources
  - Selecting best sources

- **Location & Access**
  - Contacting experts
  - Using special subject resources
- **Use of Information**
  - Note taking and crediting sources
  - Use of citation making tools
  - Beyond copy and paste
- **Synthesis**
  - Combining information from multiple sources
  - Options for presentation
  - Formal writing or presenting styles (i.e., less use of the first person)
  - Outlining or storyboarding a presentation
  - Citing in context (relate to Use of Information as well)
- **Evaluation**
  - Tips and techniques for effective presentations
  - How to save time and effort
  - Understanding rubrics and criteria
  - Self-assessment

It is valuable to have these mini-lessons available if students have questions or difficulties in one or more of these areas.

Measured

Rubrics

Rubrics or "scoring guides" provide a straightforward structure for outlining assessment criteria and levels for assignments. Rubrics can be applied to content learning as well as skills attainment.

For example, the Washington State classroom-based assessment titled "You Decide" is a culminating assignment that challenges students to use the information problem-solving skills they developed throughout the year. Students must state a position on a public issue, provide background on two positions on the issue, explain how the position relates to a right or the common good, and list two sources (see Figure 10.5).

The accompanying rubric for "You Decide" (see Figure 10.6) is directly tied to specific state social studies content standards (referred to as grade level expectations [GLE] and essential academic learning requirements [EALR]) and delineates four levels of achievement, from 4, Excellent, to 1, Minimal. The grade level expectations clearly focus on learning civics concepts and skills, for example, 5.4.1 and 5.3.1, to take a position on a public issue and relate the issue to rights and the common good. However, the 5.4.1 GLE also includes "researches multiple perspectives," and 5.4.2 has "prepares a list of resources," which directly reflect information seeking strategies, location & access, use of information, and synthesis.

The Big6 stages provide an inclusive framework for a self-assessment rubric that requires students to focus on how well they accomplished each stage of the process (see Figure 10.7 and also Chapter 9).

Elementary School Recommended for 5th Grade

You Decide CBA

Citizens in a democracy have the right and responsibility to make informed decisions. You will make an informed decision on a public issue after researching and discussing different perspectives on this issue.

Directions to Students[1]

In a cohesive paper or presentation[2], you will:

- ☐ State a position on a public issue.
- ☐ Provide background on the issue by explaining two stakeholders' positions on this issue.
- ☐ Include an explanation of how EITHER a right OR the common good relates to the position on the issue.
- ☐ List two sources including the title, author, type of source, and date of each source.

[1] This directions page guides students towards the "proficient" level (level "3") for this CBA. To help students reach "excellent" (level "4"), please refer to the rubric or, if available, the graphic organizer.
[2] Students may do a paper or presentation in response to the CBA provided that for either format, there is documentation of this response that someone outside their classroom could easily understand and review using the rubric (e.g., a videotaped presentation, an electronic written document).

www.k12.wa.us/SocialStudies/Assessments/Elementary/ElemCivics-YouDecide-CBA.pdf

Figure 10.5 Washington State "You Decide" Classroom-Based Assessment

Elementary – You Decide CBA Rubric *(Recommended for 5ᵗʰ Grade*)*

GLE (EALR)	4 - Excellent	3 – Proficient	2 - Partial	1 - Minimal
	←---PASSING		NOT PASSING ---→	
5.4.1. Researches multiple perspectives to take a position on a public or historical issue in a paper or presentation. (5ᵗʰ Grade) (EALR 5.4. Creates a product…)	States a position on a public issue and concludes with a call to action***.	States a position on a public issue.	States a position on a public issue that is unclear.	Provides reasons for a possible position but does not state a position.
5.3.1. Engages others in discussions that attempt to clarify and address multiple viewpoints on public issues based on democratic ideals. (EALR 5.3 Deliberates public issues.)	Provides background on the issue by explaining**: • **Three or more** stakeholders' positions on this issue.	Provides background on the issue by explaining**: • **Two** stakeholders' positions on this issue.	Provides background on the issue by explaining**: • **One** stakeholder's position on this issue.	Provides background on the issue without explaining any stakeholder's position on the issue.
1.1.2. Evaluates how a public issue is related to constitutional rights and the common good. (5ᵗʰ Grade) (EALR 1.1. Understands key ideals and principles…) 1.4.1. Understands that civic participation involves being informed about how public issues are related to rights and responsibilities. (5ᵗʰ Grade) (EALR 1.4. Understands civic involvement)	Provides reason(s) for the position supported by evidence. The evidence includes: • An explanation of how a right relates to the position on the issue. AND • An explanation of how the common good relates to the position on the issue.	Provides reason(s) for the position supported by evidence. The evidence includes: • An explanation of how a right relates to the position on the issue. OR • An explanation of how the common good relates to the position on the issue.	• Provides reason(s) for the position with supporting evidence but WITHOUT relating the position to a right or the common good.	Provides reason(s) for the position without any supporting evidence.
5.4.2. Prepares a list of resources including the title, author, type of source, date published, and publisher for each source and arranges the sources alphabetically. (5ᵗʰ Grade) (EALR 5.4. Creates a product…)	Lists **three** sources including the title, author, type of source, and date of each source.	Lists **two** sources including the title, author, type of source, and date of each source.	Lists **one** source including the title, author, type of source, and date of the source.	Lists source(s) but does not include the title, author, type of source, and date of the source for any of them.

*OSPI recommends that this CBA be used at a particular grade level and thus, the GLEs included in the rubric are for that grade. However, if the CBA is used at another grade level within the grade band (3-5, 6-8, or 9-12), the GLEs may need to change to match the appropriate content.
** For the purposes of this rubric, "explaining" requires students to provide specific details AND commentary for each stakeholder's position.
*** If a student chooses a historical issue to analyze, she/he can include "a discussion of how this issue helps understand current issues" rather than "a call to action."

www.k12.wa.us/SocialStudies/Assessments/Elementary/ElemCivics-YouDecide-CBA.pdf

Figure 10.6 Rubric for Classroom-Based Assessment (5th-Grade Civics)

Big6™ Skill	Yes (2)	Almost (1)	No (0)
1. Task Definition 1.1 I defined the information problem. 1.2 I identified the information needed.			
2. Information Seeking Strategies 2.1 I determined all possible sources. 2.2 I selected the best sources.			
3. Location & Access 3.1 I located sources. 3.2 I found information within sources.			
4. Use of Information 4.1 I engaged the information (e.g., read, hear, view, touch). 4.2 I extracted relevant information.			
5. Synthesis 5.1 I organized from multiple sources. 5.2 I presented the information.			
I need to work on:			
I really like:			

Compiled by Colet Bartow. Big6 by the Month: Evaluation (2012).

Figure 10.7 Sample Self-Assessment Instrument (All Big6™ Skills)

Assessment Planning

Consider assessment strategies *before* the assignment is given to students. This approach is sometimes called "backward design" and is detailed in Jay McTighe and Grant Wiggins's *Understanding by Design* (http://shop.ascd .org/Default.aspx?TabID=55&ProductId=406&Understanding-by-design-expanded-2nd-edition). A unit plan based on the backward design model contains the elements outlined in Figure 10.8.

Teachers might also use a planning grid to identify the evidence and criteria to include in a student portfolio (see Figure 10.9 and the corresponding template in the appendices).

It's important to be strategic and targeted in choosing evidence to assess student performance. Whenever possible, use existing assignments, classwork, and homework as evidence for assessing Big6 skills and subskills. As emphasized throughout this book, the Big6 is applicable to any information problem-solving activity. That's why it is possible and desirable to measure performance on Big6 skills and subskills based on evidence that is already collected and available.

The Big6 can also be used to guide students' discussion of their learning in student-led conferences or other end-of-year opportunities for students to present and reflect on what they've learned. Include the power grade level objectives, the evidence used to demonstrate student learning, and the criteria for success. Grade level learning objectives from each month should drive selection of evidence. The criteria should align with the learning objective and be clearly reflected in the evidence.

Finally, student portfolios are rich sources of evidence of Big6 learning. Formally identifying Big6 information skills learning within student portfolios can be a valuable tool for communicating to parents, other teachers, and administrators about the skills and techniques that students have gained.

Unit Plan		
Desired Results	Big6 Culminating Activities	Content Standards
	Enduring Understandings	Essential Questions
Assessment Evidence	Performance Tasks	Content Assessment
	Information Skills Assessment/Performance Rubric	Evidence
Learning Plan	Lesson Progression	Materials and Resources
	Websites/Reference	Other Details

Compiled by Colet Bartow. Big6 by the Month: Culminating Activities (2013).

Figure 10.8 Sample Unit Plan

Big6™	Power Grade Level Objectives	Evidence	Criteria
Task Definition			
Information Seeking Strategies			
Location & Access			
Use of Information			
Synthesis			
Evaluation			

Compiled by Colet Bartow. Big6 by the Month: Culminating Activities (2012).

Figure 10.9 Planning Grid for Evidence and Criteria

Evaluate Instruction

Measurement also relates to assessing your own performance as a teacher of information and technology skills. Barbara Jansen ("Evaluating Big6 Units") suggests evaluating your delivery of Big6 units by answering the following questions:

- How successful was this Big6 unit? Will you teach it again?
- How successful was the level of student engagement?
- How effectively were the learning objectives or standards met?
- What do you need to consider or change the next time you teach this unit?

These questions reflect criteria that can be applied to any instructional unit that includes formal Big6 instruction.

Reported

Culminating activities offer rich evidence to share with students, other teachers and administrators, and parents about student performance and the overall Big6 program.

TRAILS

The TRAILS assessment program, discussed in earlier chapters, provides various reports on performance that can be used (see Figure 10.10).

Teachers and administrators use the class report to assess learning and plan for future instruction. Combine class report data into spreadsheets for each grade level to facilitate overall planning for classroom teachers, teacher-librarians, and administrators. As classes move on to the next grade level, any gap in information skills can be addressed, because this type of summative assessment data is available.

Student reports provide data on individual student performance. Use student report data to assign grades on units and even on report cards.

The online review offers students valuable feedback about their performance, particularly about areas that need improvement. The online interactions also serve as a learning mechanism, as students see the correct responses.

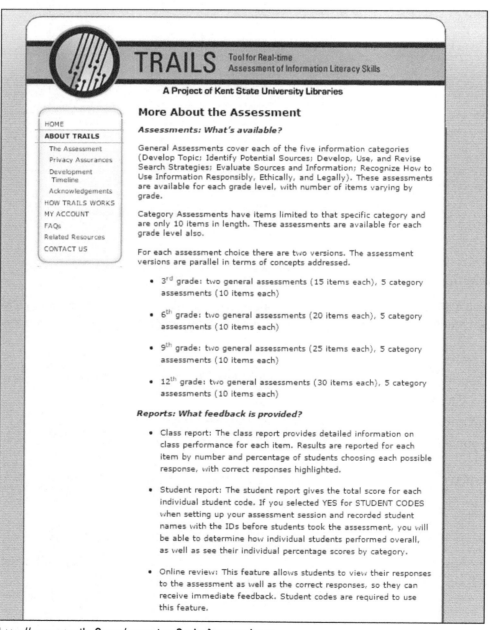

http://www.trails-9.org/overview2.php?page=about

Figure 10.10 TRAILS Reports

Report to Parents

The Big6 by the Month program emphasizes continual communication with parents about their children's academic goals, activities, and information and technology skills attainment. We believe strongly that ICT learning is essential for every student and is as important as the mainstream subject areas of language arts, mathematics, social studies, and science. Therefore, we have a responsibility to see that all students gain essential Big6 skills and that their parents are fully informed about student achievement and needs.

Parents and caregivers benefit from specific information we can provide that will help them to help their children succeed. Figure 10.11 offers a culminating report to parents that includes questions parents can use to engage in more

Sample Message for May–June	Students have focused on:	Questions to ask:
Dear Parents/Guardians: During the months of May and June, your student will work on a variety of projects and assignments. As part of each project, we will focus on a review of the Big6™ information problem-solving process. You can help reinforce these skills by asking your student questions that relate to each of the stages: Task Definition Information Seeking Strategies Location & Access Use of Information Synthesis Evaluation The chart in this message details the skills students will practice and some questions you can ask to help students be successful as they complete assignments and projects. Please contact me if you have any questions. Sincerely, [provide contact information]	Task Definition	1. How do you "define" problems? 2. What strategies do you use to identify needed information?
	Information Seeking Strategies	1. What strategies do you use to determine all possible sources? 2. How do you decide the best sources to use?
	Location & Access	1. What tools do you use to locate sources? 2. What strategies and tools do you use to locate information within sources?
	Use of Information	1. What is your preferred way to engage with new information: read, view, or listen? 2. How do you know when you've found the most relevant information?
	Synthesis	1. What strategies do you use to organize information? 2. How do you choose the best method to present your results?
	Evaluation	1. What project or presentation was your favorite? 2. What part of the Big6 process is your favorite?

Big6 by the Month: Culminating Activities (2013). Developed by Colet Bartow.

Figure 10.11 Sample Report to Parents, Review of Big6™

productive conversations about what students are expected to know and be able to do. We emphasize parent- and student-friendly language and encourage teachers to take time to explain to students and parents about what these stages mean. The important thing is to encourage conversation between parents and students. These conversations serve to reinforce the skills of self-evaluation and allow students to share their learning with confidence.

Checklists for Educators

In the appendix we offer a range of checklists and templates to help evaluate delivery of the Big6 by the Month program as well as to plan for next year. The templates and checklists help teachers to gather standards, create grade level objectives, plan lessons, plan a program, and create rubrics and self-assessment instruments. Various tools and figures offered throughout this book (e.g., Figure 10.7) can also be used to gather, organize, and evaluate information about the program for planning purposes.

Summary

The Big6 by the Month program concludes the year with culminating activities in the months of May and June. Culminating activities directly address ICT literacy and Common Core standards related to final research projects and papers. These culminating projects are intended to help students integrate various skills, techniques, and tools into the full Super3 and Big6 processes. Metacognition—being aware of one's own styles of learning and knowing—is very powerful, and culminating activities help students gain this self-awareness.

Culminating activities also provide end-of-the-year opportunities for review and improvement of students' abilities in each of the Big6 stages and to determine needs and approaches for future years.

Each element of the Big6 by the Month program—Defined, Predictable, Measured, and Reported—contributes to effective culminating experiences that improve student learning and performance.

Online Resources

Useful Sites: Assignment Organizers

Barbara Jansen, Assignment Organizer for Grades 7–12, http://library.sasaustin.org/assignmentOrganizer.php

Research Paper Organizer, http://library.sasaustin.org/paperOrganizerUS.php

Research Assistant, http://library.sasaustin.org/researchAssistant.php

Useful Sites: Culminating Projects

OSPI-Developed Assessments in Social Studies, the Arts, Health and Fitness, and Educational Technology, http://www.k12.wa.us/assessment/OSPI-DevelopedAssessments.aspx

Sample Culminating Projects (WA OSPI), http://www.k12.wa.us/GraduationRequirements/CulminatingProjects/default.aspx

Useful Site: Assessment

TRAILS: Tools for Real-Time Assessment of Information Literacy Skills, http://www.trails-9.org/

Useful Site: Evaluating Instruction

"Evaluating Big6 Units" by Barbara Jansen. http://big6.com/media/freestuff/Evaluating_Big6_Units.pdf

Chapter 11

"PLAN IT FORWARD"
Looking Ahead

In This Chapter

❑ Conclusion: Status of Your Comprehensive Big6™ by the Month Program

❑ Plans for Next Year

❑ Summary

Conclusion: Status of Your Comprehensive Big6™ by the Month Program

We hope we've been clear and consistent from the beginning and throughout this book about our prime and foundational conviction:

> **There is nothing more important to student success in school and life than information and communication technology literacy.**

Certainly we recognize that reading, writing, and mathematical competence are essential. We don't question the importance and value of science, social studies, art, music, and other subject areas.

But there is nothing—NOTHING—more fundamental to human success and achievement in any endeavor than being able to size up a task or problem from an information perspective and then to be able to find, use, evaluate, and process information to address that task or problem. These are information skills. That's what it means to be information literate.

While we don't think that many would disagree with this fundamental conviction, we are frustrated and dismayed to realize that few K–12 schools or districts truly address it with instructional programs that reach every student. We know that many schools offer some form of information or research skills instruction, but few if any offer comprehensive programs that reach every student.

That's what this book and the Big6 by the Month program are all about: helping every student in every school attain the essential ICT literacy skills necessary to be successful in anything they choose to do. And if you have read through this entire book or gone through the Big6 by the Month program with us, we know that you too accept the challenge of ensuring that every student is ICT literate.

We have worked together to fulfill the promise of providing *comprehensive* information and communication technology (ICT) literacy programs for every student in every school. Together, we have tried to design, develop, and deliver a comprehensive program that is the following:

- *Defined* in terms of the goals and specific skills and knowledge that students are expected to learn.

- *Predictable* in terms of how and when students are to learn the defined, essential information and technology skills and knowledge.

- *Measurable* in terms of setting accountable goals for the program and assessing performance by the students.

- *Reported* to students and parents and to other teachers, administrators, and decision makers.

In developing the Big6 by the Month program and working with you, we have learned that there are many barriers and roadblocks to overcome. Teachers and schools are overwhelmed with requirements, testing, new mandates, tight schedules, lack of resources, stretched faculty, and more. But we've also found opportunities and the means to move forward: cooperative teacher colleagues, information-rich assignments, connections to the Common Core and other standards.

We've designed the Big6 by the Month program to stay true to its central purpose of reaching every student but also to be flexible and adaptable to local situations and constraints.

For example, if you are a classroom teacher in a school that does not have a school-wide information literacy program, you can still engage in defining a set of Super3 or Big6 standards to address each month; assess student performance; and communicate progress to the students, other teachers and administrators, and parents.

Or, if you are a teacher-librarian or technology teacher with scheduled classes, you too can define monthly Big6 or Super3 standards, link to classroom units or assignments, deliver appropriate lessons, assess progress, and report widely.

At any level (classroom, library, or lab, in elementary, secondary, or higher education) or setting (school, district, region, state, or country), the Big6 by the Month program provides a structure and approach for developing a program to reach every student. You can start small: one or two lessons per month addressing one or two power objectives per class or grade. But Big6 by the Month also facilitates developing school-, district-, or statewide programs.

We are certain that each of you has attained some success in your own Big6 by the Month program. We encourage you to reflect on each element of the process—Defined, Predictable, Measured, Reported; document the standards addressed and activities engaged in; communicate to other educators, parents, and the public; and begin to revise and plan for next year.

Here are some guidelines to help you in this reflection. These points and questions can be useful for personal consideration or for group or team discussions:

- **Defined:** Identify and describe the number and scope of standards addressed each month for each Super3 or Big6 skill for each grade level or teacher. What school or district priorities were you able to focus on (e.g., Common Core State Standards)? What were the strengths of your program, and what might be improved?

- **Predictable:** Identify and describe the monthly program. Did you follow the Big6 by the Month calendar, or did you make adjustments? How many lessons were offered to each class, and who delivered the lessons? Can you provide a summary chart or table of lessons, evidence, and assessment results for grade levels or individual classes over the course of the school year? Was the instruction reinforced across multiple settings, that is, library, labs, classroom, community? What worked well, and what might be improved or expanded next year?

- **Measured:** Identify and describe the range of measurements and student performance. What forms of assessment were used each month? How were assessments integrated with classroom activities, assignments, and homework? Did students engage in self-assessment? Was there a connection to school-, district-, or statewide tests? Were culminating assessments used? What worked well, and what needs to be addressed for next year?

- **Reported:** Identify and describe communication and reporting efforts. Include an example of monthly reports. Is there a line item on report cards for information skills or ICT literacy? What techniques were used to inform students of their performance? How did you reach out to parents and the community? Did you report regularly to administrators and other teachers? Did you use new technologies (e.g., website, blogs, social media) in reporting? What forms of reporting worked well, and what might be improved or expanded next year?

Pulling together information for these elements and then analyzing and reflecting should provide rich content for your end-of-the-year report to administration. We also recommend considering a short, verbal report to faculty at a faculty meeting in May or June. We know that this can be somewhat time-consuming, but the payoff can be huge—in gaining awareness and recognition of the program, building support, and gaining resources and infrastructure.

Plans for Next Year

We have stressed the value of systematic and careful planning for your Big6 by the Month program. Here we provide some additional content to help you revise and expand existing plans based on the needs of students and other educators.

The framework for all plans is the predictable Big6 by the Month schedule. We encourage you to stick with our common calendar if possible (see Figure 11.1) so that we can build a global, Big6 by the Month presence as well as share lessons, assessments, templates, and even planning documents.

September	Overview
October	Task Definition
November	Information Seeking Strategies
December	Location & Access
January	Use of Information
February	Review and Reflect
March	Synthesis
April	Evaluation
May	Culminating Activities

Figure 11.1 Big6™ by the Month Calendar

We recognize that this might not be possible due to local or regional requirements or routines. If so, we still encourage you to reach out to others in your school or district to set up a common, local Big6 calendar that can be shared, publicized, and highlighted continually.

Another useful tool is the *Scenario Planning Template* (see Figure 11.2), which helps in laying out the opportunities and constraints of your situation so that you can develop a plan that is realistic and doable in your situation. Review the items in the second or middle column and revise or add as appropriate for your situation. Use the third column to enter data about your situation. The first three rows should establish the baseline of your situation and affect the content of the last row (Result).

The final figure offered here (Figure 11.3) provides a quick guideline for lesson development related to the 12 Big6 substages. This figure is not comprehensive, but it is provided to show how the Big6 can easily translate into valuable lessons on specific skills, tools, or techniques.

Information Literacy Goals	Power Grade Level Objectives • per grade Lessons • per day/week/month	
Capacity	Teaching • Teacher/Librarian • Technology Teacher • Classroom/Subject Teacher • Other (e.g., online)	
Means	Lessons Delivered • Daily/Weekly • Classroom-based • Library-based • Technology-based • Other	
Result	Lessons Delivered • no. per grade • no. per day/week/month • assessment	

Figure 11.2 Scenario Planning Template

Big6™ Stage	Substages	Lesson Focus Ideas
1. Task Definition	1.1 Define the information problem.	Choose a topic. Frame a question. Identify keywords. Make a plan. Use graphic organizers.
	1.2 Identify types of information needed.	Consider types and amount of information • Facts • Opinions • Statistics • Graphs • Pictures
2. Information Seeking Strategies	2.1 Determine all possible sources.	Article databases World Wide Web Books People

Big6™ Stage	Substages	Lesson Focus Ideas
	2.2 Select the best sources.	Reliable Authoritative Current Objective Relevant Easy to use Available Fun
3. Location & Access	3.1 Locate sources.	Search engine Databases Online catalog Advanced search strategies
	3.2 Find information within sources.	Indexes Directories Tables of contents Glossaries Keywords Skim and scan
4. Use of Information	4.1 Engage the information.	Read for purpose. Skim and scan. Identify main ideas.
	4.2 Extract relevant information.	Take notes. Cite sources. Distinguish among quote, paraphrase, and summary.
5. Synthesis	5.1 Organize the information.	Sort notes. Use graphic organizers.
	5.2 Present the information.	Identify audience. Consider variety of formats. Cite sources.
6. Evaluation	6.1 Judge the product.	Use rubrics to self-assess. Compare to teacher and peer evaluations.
	6.2 Judge the process.	Examine task completion process (time management, self-regulation, etc.). Identify areas for improvement.

Figure 11.3 Selected Lesson Focus Ideas for Each Big6™ Stage

Summary

And that's the full scope of the Big6 by the Month program! We've attempted to provide a strong conceptual underpinning for planning and delivering highly valuable programs. While the specifics of standards, lessons, assessments, and reports will change, the overall systematic approach of defined, predictable, measured, and reported should continue to be widely applicable and effective.

We've learned a lot in creating this program and will continue to learn. Please continue to work with us through the online Big6 by the Month website (https://sites.google.com/site/big6xthemonth/) and discussion group (https:// groups.google.com/forum/#!forum/b6month).

We sincerely appreciate your enthusiasm for the Super3 and Big6 and this program to better prepare young people through ICT literacy for the challenges and opportunities of living in our information-centric and increasingly digital world.

APPENDICES

GLOSSARY

assessment. The measurement of student performance compared to the expectations outlined in the standards. Assessment of student success should rely on multiple measures of student work through performance tasks, self-assessments, regular feedback from teachers, feedback from peers, and tests. <Montana Office of Public Instruction. Curriculum Development Guide. *http://opi.mt.gov/Curriculum/Curriculum-Development-Guide/*>

assignment organizer. A tool that helps students approach an assignment by specifying sequential steps.

Big6™ Skills. A program that integrates information search and use skills along with technology tools in a systematic process to find, use, apply, and evaluate information for specific needs and tasks. <*http://big6.com/pages/about /big6-skills-overview.php*>

Boolean logic. A system derived from a mathematical logic system developed by George Boole; used in Internet searching by combining words with AND, OR, and NOT to retrieve more targeted results. <*http://edmc.lib answers.com/a.php?qid=792208*>

browse. To view or search somewhat randomly, as in a store or library. <*http://dictionary.reference.com/browse /browse?s=t*>

content standards. The agreed-upon requirements that describe what students need to know and be able to do in a particular curricular area.

criteria. The characteristics used to evaluate success.

curriculum. A set of courses, based on standards, that provides a roadmap to guide teacher planning of instruction, regular assessment of student learning, sequencing of units and lessons, and resources needed to support student success. <Montana Office of Public Instruction. Curriculum Development Guide. *http://opi.mt.gov/Curriculum /Curriculum-Development-Guide/*>

curriculum map. An outline of the implemented curriculum; what is taught and when it is actually taught.

delivery-centered instruction. Traditional instruction delivered by an individual.

evidence. Samples of student performance.

formative assessment. A means to monitor student performance to provide ongoing feedback during the learning process. <"Teaching Excellence and Educational Innovation," Carnegie Mellon University. *http://www.cmu.edu /teaching/index.html*>

grade level objectives. The knowledge and skills one wants students in a grade to acquire by the end of an activity or teaching unit. <"Teaching Excellence and Educational Innovation," Carnegie Mellon University. *http://www.cmu .edu/teaching/index.html*>

ICT literacy. *See* information and communication technology literacy.

Information and communication technology (ICT) literacy. The ability to efficiently use digital technologies and networking tools to access, evaluate, organize, integrate, and create information. <Partnership for 21st Century Learning *http://www.p21.org/storage/documents/docs/P21_Framework_Definitions_New_Logo_2015.pdf*>

information literacy. Category that encompasses ICT literacy.

learning expectations. Objectives that define the knowledge and skills one wants students to acquire by the end of an activity or teaching unit. <"Teaching Excellence and Educational Innovation," Carnegie Mellon University. *http://www.cmu.edu/teaching/index.html*>

levels of performance. A rating system that assesses achievement by describing degrees of mastery. <"Teaching Excellence and Educational Innovation," Carnegie Mellon University. *http://www.cmu.edu/teaching/index.html*>

management-centered instruction. A teaching arrangement in which someone provides structure and guidance to the person who will deliver the instruction.

objectives. The knowledge and skills one wants students to acquire by the end of a learning activity. <"Teaching Excellence and Educational Innovation," Carnegie Mellon University. *http://www.cmu.edu/teaching/index.html*>

paraphrase. To rewrite a passage from source material in one's own words. The source must be cited, and paraphrased material is usually shorter than the original. <"Quoting, Paraphrasing and Summarizing," Purdue Online Writing Lab. *http://owl.english.purdue.edu/owl/resource/563/1/*>

performance descriptors. Words or phrases that state how well and at what level students apply knowledge and demonstrate skills defined by standards and learning objectives. Performance may be described on a continuum from novice to advanced, beginner to expert, or basic to sophisticated. <Montana Office of Public Instruction. Content Standards Framework. Curriculum Development Guide. *http://opi.mt.gov/Curriculum/Curriculum-Development-Guide/*>

performance rubric. A set of criteria describing students' performance, along a continuum from advanced to novice, that define how well they apply the knowledge and skills contained in essential learning expectations. Rubrics can be generalized and analytical or task-specific and pinpoint a particular skill.

quotation. A passage from a source that is copied verbatim. Its source must be cited precisely. <"Quoting, Paraphrasing and Summarizing," Purdue Online Writing Lab. *http://owl.english.purdue.edu/owl/resource/563/1/*>

research. Diligent and systematic inquiry or investigation into a subject. <*http://dictionary.reference.com/browse/research?s=t*>

rubric. A scoring tool that explicitly describes the instructor's performance expectations for an assignment, with values assigned.

search. The purposeful attempt to find information to answer a question or solve a problem.

search techniques. Methods for locating information. Strategies include use of keywords, Boolean logic, phrases, skimming, and scanning. <Montana Office of Public Instruction. "Essential Learning Expectations for Information Literacy." *http://www.opi.mt.gov/pdf/Standards/10FebELE_LibMedia.xls*>

search tools. Features of text or digital sources that help students locate information within and across such sources (e.g., database search interfaces, subject directories, digital indexes, glossaries, tables of contents). <Montana Office of Public Instruction. "Essential Learning Expectations for Information Literacy." *http://www.opi.mt.gov/pdf/Standards/10FebELE_LibMedia.xls*>

standards. Agreed-upon requirements for what students need to know and be able to do.

summary. A short restatement of information from source material, highlighting the main ideas. The source must be cited. <"Quoting, Paraphrasing and Summarizing," Purdue Online Writing Lab. *http://owl.english.purdue.edu/owl/resource/563/1/*>

summative assessment. An evaluation of student learning at the end of an instructional unit by comparing it to some standard or benchmark. <"Teaching Excellence and Educational Innovation," Carnegie Mellon University. *http://www.cmu.edu/teaching/index.html*>

Super3™. A program that contains the same basic elements as the Big6 program but is offered in language that is easy for very young students to understand. Students in grades K–2 learn the basics—Plan, Do, Review—and prepare to apply a process approach to assignments. <*http://big6.com/media/freestuff/Big6Handouts.pdf*>

BIG6™ BY THE MONTH

Webinars Recordings Archive 2013–2014 (last updated 04/24/14)

Presented by Mike Eisenberg, Janet Murray, and Colet Bartow, with Sue Wurster

Big6 by the Month offers the conceptual and practical foundation to help you plan and deliver an information and communication technology literacy instructional program that is comprehensive, predictable, and accountable. Use the links and password information below to listen to each recorded webinar.

Recorded Webinars:

1. Big6 by the Month: Overview recording: https://vimeo.com/72978630 (no password assigned)

2. Big6 by the Month, Task Definition recording: https://vimeo.com/75063701 Password: b6xmtd2013

3. Big6 by the Month, Information Seeking Strategies recording: https://vimeo.com/77184390 Password: b6xmiss1013w

4. Big6 by the Month, Location & Access recording: https://vimeo.com/80039990 Password: LA111321

5. Big6 by the Month, Use of Information: https://vimeo.com/81824337 Password: USE131212

6. Big6 by the Month, Revisit and Reflect: https://vimeo.com/84415603 Password: b6xmSurvey

7. Big6 by the Month, Synthesis (February 20, 2014): https://vimeo.com/90273982 Password: b6xmsyn2202

8. Big6 by the Month, Evaluation (March 20, 2014): https://vimeo.com/90070034 Password: b6xm420146

9. Big6 by the Month, Culminating Activities (April 24, 2014): https://vimeo.com/93562626 Password: B6CA41424

TEMPLATES

Standards Template

Look at **your** state's content standards at **http://www.educationworld.com/standards/** and/or **http://www .corestandards.org/read-the-standards/**. Fill in standards related to each **Big6** stage.

State:	Source (URL):
Language Arts:	
Social Studies:	
Science:	
Other:	
Other:	
Information Literacy: (source: _____)	

© Big6™ by the Month (2013). The Big6 is © Michael B. Eisenberg and Robert E. Berkowitz. Big6 Associates, LLC, www.big6.com.

From *The Big6 Curriculum: Comprehensive Information and Communication Technology (ICT) Literacy for All Students* by Michael B. Eisenberg, Janet Murray, and Colet Bartow. Santa Barbara, CA: Libraries Unlimited. Copyright © 2016.

Grade Level Objectives Template

Big6™ Stage:	Month:
Related content standard:	Cross grade level objective:
Grade _____	
Grade _____	
Grade _____	
Grade _____	
Grade _____	

Annual Grade Level Plan Template

Grade: _____

Month	AGENDA Super3™/Big6™	Stage	GRADE LEVEL OBJECTIVES	CLASSROOM ASSIGNMENTS/ UNITS
Sept	Overview: The process			
Oct	PLAN Task Definition	1.1 1.2		
Nov	PLAN Info Seeking Strategies	2.1 2.2		
Dec	DO Location & Access	3.1 3.2		
Jan	DO Use of Information	4.1 4.2		
Feb	Revisit/Reflect			
Mar	DO Synthesis	5.1 5.2		
Apr	REVIEW Evaluation	6.1 6.2		
May	Culminating Activities/ Events		Complete a major subject area assignment	

Scenario Plan Template

Information Literacy Goals	Power Grade Level Objectives: – per grade Lessons: – per day/week/month	
Capacity	Teaching: – Teacher-Librarian – Technology Teacher – Classroom/Subject Teacher – Other (e.g., online)	
Means	Lessons Delivered: – Daily/Weekly – Classroom-based – Library-based – Technology-based – Other	
Result	Lessons Delivered: – no. per grade – no. per day/week/month – assessment	

Program Plan Template

Your School:	Number of students:
Grade levels:	Number of teachers (total):
Subject areas:	Number of teachers per grade:
For each grade, identify requisite classes/teachers required to reach every student in that grade in a 2 week span.	Grade:
Grade:	Grade:
*Provide mini-lessons on **Big6 stage** _____ in _____ to:* *(month)*	Teacher/Grade/Subject Area:
Teacher/Grade/Subject Area:	Teacher/Grade/Subject Area:
Provide direct instruction in the library to:	Teacher/Grade/Subject Area:
Teacher/Grade/Subject Area:	Teacher/Grade/Subject Area:
Alternative delivery (e.g., technology teacher, online):	
Total number of students receiving instruction:	Total number of lessons delivered:

From *The Big6 Curriculum: Comprehensive Information and Communication Technology (ICT) Literacy for All Students* by Michael B. Eisenberg, Janet Murray, and Colet Bartow. Santa Barbara, CA: Libraries Unlimited. Copyright © 2016.

Lesson Plan Template

Big6™ Stage:	Subject Area:
Grade Level:	Lesson Focus:
Grade Level Objective:	Content Standard(s):

Learning Activity:

Assessment Evidence:	Assessment Criteria:

Unit Plan Template

(based on Wiggins and McTighe, *Understanding by Design*)

Desired Results	Big6™ Stage	Content Standards
	Enduring Understandings	Essential Questions
Assessment Evidence	Performance Tasks	Content Assessment
	Information Skills Assessment/Performance Rubric	Evidence
Learning Plan	Lesson Progression	Materials and Resources
	Websites/Reference	Other Details

From *The Big6 Curriculum: Comprehensive Information and Communication Technology (ICT) Literacy for All Students* by Michael B. Eisenberg, Janet Murray, and Colet Bartow. Santa Barbara, CA: Libraries Unlimited. Copyright © 2016.

Summary Evidence and Criteria Template

Big6™ Skill	*Power Grade* **Level Objectives**	Evidence	Criteria
Task Definition			
Information Seeking Strategies			
Location & Access			
Use of Information			
Synthesis			
Evaluation			

Performance Descriptors Template

Performance descriptors should incorporate *criteria* based on the learning objectives to clearly indicate the path to success. Criteria often reflect degrees of completeness, accuracy, and frequency of display. The language in a performance description should be specific to the grade level and readily accessible to students and parents.

Big6™ Stage:		Evidence:		Grade:
Criteria	Novice	Nearing Proficient	Proficient	Advanced

From *The Big6 Curriculum: Comprehensive Information and Communication Technology (ICT) Literacy for All Students* by Michael B. Eisenberg, Janet Murray, and Colet Bartow. Santa Barbara, CA: Libraries Unlimited. Copyright © 2016.

Sample for Big6™ 4.2 Extract Information—Grade 4

Novice	Nearing Proficient	Proficient	Advanced
Omits most details, facts, or concepts when compiling information, and/or includes many irrelevant details.	Omits some details, facts, or concepts when compiling information, and/or includes some irrelevant details.	Compiles information (note taking, graphic organizers, etc.).	Gleans new insight from details, facts, and concepts when compiling information.
All notes do not reflect a creative use of words and are not written using 4th-grade language and vocabulary. Rubistar rubric ID: 1641653	Most notes do not reflect a creative use of words and are not written using 4th-grade language and vocabulary.	Most notes reflect a creative use of words and are written using 4th-grade language and vocabulary.	All notes reflect a creative use of words and are written using 4th-grade or more advanced language and vocabulary.

© Big6™ by the Month: Use of Information (2012). Developed by Colet Bartow. The Big6 is © Michael B. Eisenberg and Robert E. Berkowitz, Big6 Associates, LLC, www.big6.com.

Sample for Big6™ 5.2 Present the Information—Grade 9–10

Criteria Gr. 9-10	Novice	Nearing Proficient	Proficient	Advanced
Create a product that presents findings.	a. Choose the medium for presentation *regardless of audience*.	a. Choose the appropriate medium for presentation with *some consideration of audience*.	a. Choose the appropriate medium for presentation *based on audience*.	a. Choose a unique medium for presentation that *clearly considers audience*.
	b. Create original product to meet *minimal* task requirements.	b. Create original product to meet *most* task requirements.	b. Create original product that meets *all* task requirements.	b. Create *high-quality* original product that meets *all* task requirements.

© Big6™ by the Month: Synthesis (2012). Developed by Colet Bartow. The Big6 is © Michael B. Eisenberg and Robert E. Berkowitz. Big6 Associates, LLC, www.big6.com.

Assignment Organizer Template

Assignment: _____ **Date Due:** _____

Complete Big6 Skills Nos. 1–5 BEFORE you BEGIN your assignment.
Complete Big6 Skill No. 6 BEFORE you TURN IN your assignment.

Big6 Skill 1: Task Definition

What does this assignment require me to do?

What information do I need in order to do this assignment?

Big6 Skill 2: Information Seeking Strategies

What sources can I use to do the assignment?
Make a list, then circle the best sources.

Big6 Skill 3: Location & Access

Where can I find my sources? Do I need help?
If so, who can help me?

Big6 Skill 4: Use of Information
What do I need to do with the information?

____ read/view/listen
____ take notes
____ answer questions
____ other: _____

____ chart and/or write an essay
____ copy and highlight
____ properly cite

Big6 Skill 5: Synthesis

What product does this assignment require?

Big6 Skill 6: Evaluation

Student self-evaluation checklist:
____ I did what I was supposed to do (see Big6 stage 1, Task Definition).
____ The assignment is complete.

Presentation Readiness Checklist

	Not Yet (0)	Yes (1)
I have identified the audience.		
I have completed each of the assignment requirements*:		
Length: no more than 15 minutes		
Format: PowerPoint presentation/video		
Catchy title: _____		
Transitions for each section		
Satisfying conclusion		
Source credits complete		

*Adapt criteria to reflect assignment requirements.

Big6™ by the Month Checklist: Instructional Leader

Month	Grade	Class

Defined
- Establish expectation for Big6 by the Month approach
- Embed Big6 by the Month in supervision process and documentation

Predictable
- Emphasize Big6 by the Month stages in each curriculum planning session or professional learning opportunity
- Provide a Big6 by the Month calendar with a curriculum map or unit planning calendar
- Provide teacher-librarian with time and opportunity to support Big6 by the Month instruction

Measured
- Establish success criteria for Big6 by the Month
- Set lesson targets for each grade level
- Track monthly lessons taught
- Compile Results
  - Lessons taught
  - Student progress
    - Pre-assessments
    - Interim assessments
    - Summative assessments

Reported
- Report Student Progress
  - Quarterly reports to parents
  - Monthly reports to district administration and trustees
- Report Teacher Results
  - Quarterly reports of grade-level lessons to teachers
  - Monthly reports to district administration and trustees

NOTES:

Big6™ by the Month Checklist: Teacher

Month	Grade	Class

Defined

- Standards Identified
- Content Area/Grade Level Expectations Chosen
- Big6 or Super3 Stage Identified

Plan		1. Task Definition	
		2. Information Seeking Strategies	
Do		3. Location & Access	
		4. Use of Information	
		5. Synthesis	
Review		6. Evaluation	

Predictable

- Curriculum Map/Unit Map Consulted
- Planning Calendar Created
- Units/Lessons Selected

Measured

- Performance Tasks Created
- Criteria Developed
  - Uses student-friendly language
  - Clear, measureable statements
- Evidence Identified

Reported

- Formative Observations and Evidence Collected
- Student-generated Evidence Collected
- Grades or Standards-based Report Generated

NOTES:

Big6™ by the Month Checklist: Teacher-Librarian

Month	Grade	Class

Defined
- Standards Identified
- Grade Level Expectations Chosen

Predictable
- Calendar for Each Grade Level Created
- Units/Lessons Selected
- Grade Level Assignments Identified
- Big6 Activities and Assessments Developed

Measured
- Criteria Developed
  - Uses student-friendly language
  - Clear, measureable statements
- Evidence Identified

Reported
- Audiences Targeted
- Format or Method Selected for Each Audience
- Frequency Determined
  - Weekly
  - Monthly
  - End of Marking Period
  - Other

NOTES:

© Big6™ by the Month (2013). Developed by Colet Bartow. The Big6 is © Michael B. Eisenberg and Robert E. Berkowitz. Big6 Associates, LLC, www.big6.com.

From *The Big6 Curriculum: Comprehensive Information and Communication Technology (ICT) Literacy for All Students* by Michael B. Eisenberg, Janet Murray, and Colet Bartow. Santa Barbara, CA: Libraries Unlimited. Copyright © 2016.

ABOUT THE AUTHORS

MICHAEL B. EISENBERG, PhD, is a teacher and mentor whose personal motto is "make it better!" He is the founding dean of the Information School at the University of Washington, serving from 1998 to 2006. During his tenure, Mike transformed the unit from a single graduate degree program into a broad-based information school with a wide range of research and academic programs. Known as a visionary and entrepreneur, Mike coined the terms "Information School" and "iSchool." Now dean emeritus and professor, the unifying aspect of his diverse management, teaching, and research activities is the ongoing effort to improve society's ability to meet people's information needs.

Mike's current work focuses on information and communication technology (ICT) literacy; mentoring faculty, information professionals, and students; and developing information schools, programs, and degrees at leading institutions of higher education. Mike is recognized as the leading global expert in information literacy. He is coauthor of the "Big6 approach to information problem-solving"—the most widely used information literacy program in the world. Mike is a prolific author (nine books and dozens of articles and papers) and has worked with thousands of students—pre-K through higher education—as well as people in business, government, and communities to improve individual and organizational information and technology access and use. Mike particularly enjoys working with undergraduate students, introducing them to the opportunities and challenges of the information field.

JANET MURRAY, MALS. By redefining the school librarian as an "Information Specialist" in terms familiar to advocates of the American Association of School Librarians' *Information Power*, the Department of Defense Dependents Schools lured Janet Murray away from the Portland (Oregon) Public Schools to Kinnick High School in Yokosuka, Japan. An early enthusiast for electronic access to information, Janet was one of the cofounders of K12Net, a global collection of bulletin board systems for educators. She was the first Telecommunications Chair and Webmaster for the Oregon Educational Media Association and served for five years as the Associate Editor for *MultiMedia Schools* magazine.

Janet Murray has been using the Big6 Skills to help middle and high school students become "information literate" since she created an online matrix and web page of activities linking the Big6 to national information literacy standards in 1999. Adding the National Educational Technology Standards for Students (NETS-S) to the matrix in 2002, she began to more deeply explore each of the Big6 Skills as they relate to standards in a series of articles for the *Big6 eNewsletter*, followed by the Linworth publication *Achieving Educational Standards Using the Big6™* (March 2008). She also codesigned and was the lead instructor for an online course using the Big6 Skills to achieve content, information literacy, and NETS standards from 2003 to 2008. Janet joined the Big6 by the Month team at its inception, manages its Google website and discussion group, and compiled the first three years of webinars to create the first draft of this book.

COLET BARTOW, MEd, is a mother, Montanan, teacher-librarian, and cheerleader for information and technology literacy. She lives in Helena, Montana, where she works for the Montana Office of Public Instruction (OPI) as Communication and Resource Coordinator for the Content Standards and Instruction division. She spent 13 years as a teacher-librarian before joining the OPI in 2007. Visit the Montana Teacher-Librarian Google site http://sites.google .com/site/montanateacherlibrarian. Follow her on Twitter (@cbartow) or make friends on Facebook, Google+, or LinkedIn.

Her first computer was a Radio Shack TRS-80, and she first held a job in a library as a third-grade student. She completed her MEd in curriculum and instruction at Montana State University and BA in English with endorsements in secondary English, school library media, and English as a second language at the University of Montana.

SUE WURSTER, BA, is an Editor and Project Manager who likes to help people achieve goals. She enjoys being part of an organization like Big6 because there is a mission; to improve human performance and productivity. Sue is a skilled communicator and good listener who enjoys using new technology to improve communications in virtual settings.

Sue first became familiar with Big6 Skills when she edited the first *Big6 Newsletters* (1994). Over the years (2001–2012) she planned and managed a range of Big6 programs, workshops, and presentations. Sue was the executive editor for all Big6 and Super3 products, including newsletters, articles, software, handbooks, worksheets, instructional materials, and websites to deliver a problem-solving approach for information and communications technology literacy skills in K–20 educational settings. She handled Big6 and Super3 training requests and contract administration with hundreds of US schools and schools in other countries. She set up and moderated many live Big6 webinar sessions by Mike Eisenberg and other Big6 trainers. Sue has been the project coordinator, editor, and webinar moderator for all Big6 by the Month webinar presentations since the project began in 2010.

Formerly, Sue was Publications Coordinator for the ERIC/IT Clearinghouse on Information and Technology at Syracuse University (1994–2001), where she planned and managed a full publication program involving frequent author communication, full editorial process, print production, and publication marketing. Sue is a graduate of Nazareth College of Rochester (BA, 1992), where she majored in English literature with a concentration in writing. Currently, Sue focuses on the Big6 by the Month project management, marketing, and business management from her virtual office in the New York State North Country region.